Climbing
Family Trees
Whispers in the Leaves

Climbing

Family Trees
Whispers in the Leaves

by
Trina Boice and Tracey Long

Spring Creek Book Company
Provo, Utah

ISBN 13: 978-1-932898-49-1
ISBN 10: 1-932898-49-2
e. 1

Published by Spring Creek Book Company
P.O. Box 50355
Provo, Utah 84605-0355
www.springcreekbooks.com

Cover design © Spring Creek Book Company
Cover design by Nicole Cunningham
Inside illustrations © Calvin W. Boice III

Printed in the United States of America
10 9 8 7 6 5 4 3 2 1
Printed on acid-free paper

Library of Congress Cataloging-in-Publication Data
Boice, Trina, 1963-
   Climbing family trees : whispers in the leaves / by Trina Boice and
Tracey Long.
     p. cm.
   Summary: "Inspirational stories from genealogists and instructions for
how to begin searching for your family history"--Provided by publisher.
   ISBN-13: 978-1-932898-49-1 (pbk. : alk. paper)
   ISBN-10: 1-932898-49-2 (pbk. : alk. paper)
   1. United States--Genealogy--Handbooks, manuals, etc. 2. Genealogy
--Religious aspects--Church of Jesus Christ of Latter-day Saints.
3. Genealogy--Anecdotes. 4. Genealogy--Poetry.   I. Long, Tracey.
II. Title.
CS47.B65 2006
929.1072073--dc22
                                    2005026941

TABLE OF CONTENTS

ACKNOWLEDGMENTS

We would like to thank all of the wonderful people who contributed their stories and heart to this book. Genealogists have an incredible giving spirit and are always so willing to help others and share the joy of doing family history. As the stories poured in, we sat at our computers with goose-bumps and shivers of joy, as a warm spirit testified to us that the veil between heaven and earth is very thin.

We would also like to thank our publisher, Chad Daybell, for believing in this project before he ever saw a written word. We truly appreciate his support and encouragement.

Big hugs and kisses to thank our parents, Jack Bates and Darla Rice Sutherland, for the wonderfully rich heritage they have given us. It has been an honor to research our family and discover the inspiring ancestors who have given us such a great legacy. It is our dream to make them proud of us and what we have done with their name.

We would also like to thank our husbands and children, who humored us while we typed madly on the computer, letting the laundry and dishes pile up. We hope that our children will cherish their heritage and add to it. Our lives are rich because of them.

We testify that the family unit is eternal. Heavenly Father is keenly aware of even our smallest efforts to research our family history and is eager to help us. The heavens must giggle as we stumble onto important genealogy information and each other. Someone once said, "A coincidence is simply a miracle where God chose to be anonymous."

Trina Bates Boice and Tracey Bates Long

P R O L O G U E

For years we would sit wide-eyed and with attentive ears to hear people share stories about their family history. We especially loved hearing stories that illustrated unseen help from above in finding ancestors. It is our belief that our ancestors are more a part of our lives than we realize. They watch, perhaps wide-eyed too, as we take our turn to walk this earth.

Surely these ancestors would love to have their faith-promoting stories told and cherished. How terribly sad for those sitting in the heavens to be forgotten by their own family! We rejoiced with each story and cheered for those valiantly seeking after their kindred dead. We sighed with those who wandered for hours in cemeteries and gulped a grateful breath when they finally found that lost ancestor. With deep emotion the stories all declared the strong message that family is the most important possession we will have in this life. It is our responsibility, duty and greatest joy to seek after and treasure our family.

There is a universal law which declares, "There is opposition in all things." We experienced it several times during the process of compiling these stories.

Not once, but TWICE (because we're twins) did our separate computer hard drives crash and engulf all our data and precious stories. If it wasn't for the fact that, as identical twins, we want copies of everything the other does, and that we received some heavenly help, you would not be reading this book today! After we each lost our hard drive, the other twin was able to recover everything from her database and share it. One of our young sons was getting curiously spooked by the fact that this book was about "the dead" and now our computers had both gone "dead." It was as if an opposing force did not want these stories to be told and shared. Forces were exerted twice to stop the publishing of these faith-promoting family stories!

There is also another universal law which states, "By small and simple things shall great things come to pass." By our small, daily persistence we were able to piece together this collection of great stories, TWICE! It is also an appropriate lesson for any genealogist to remember; that by small, persistent steps one can climb the monumental family tree. Digging for your family roots implies a head looking downward into the dirt. We prefer the phrase "Climbing your Family Tree," which creates the visual image of looking upward through your ascent... and that's exactly where the help comes from.

We hope you enjoy these stories . . . we have twice!

CHAPTER 1

Digging for Our Roots
Why climb your family tree?

Someone once said, "If you want to have spiritual experiences, do your genealogy." There is something magical and unusually compelling about genealogy. Unlike playing golf or doing crafts or participating in any other pastime, researching our family history is something sacred that calls to us. There is a special something that tugs at the genealogist's heart and pulls him to keep searching through dusty books and rolls of microfiche late into the night. You may be a professional genealogist or just a beginner trying to find a long lost cousin on the Internet. Your search may originate from curiosity, duty, or even religious dedication, but either way, you have felt that ancestral tug.

The search for one's roots became an increasingly popular hobby, thanks to Alex Haley's Pulitzer Prize winning book *Roots* and the subsequent 1975 TV miniseries, which fascinated viewers as they watched the story of a family unfold from the shores of Africa to the slave plantations in America. Alex Haley explained it well when he said,

"In all of us there is a hunger, marrow deep, to know our heritage—to know who we are and where we have come from. Without this enriching knowledge, there is a hollow yearning. No matter what our attainments in this life, there is still a vacuum, an emptiness, and the most disquieting loneliness." (What Roots Means to Me," *Readers Digest*, May 1977). People want to know where they come from and feel like they are connected to something bigger than themselves.

The Climb

As we listen to the voices whispering in the leaves of our family tree, we can hear the secrets of our own lives. They are the whispers of our ancestors who have paved the way for us. They often reveal us to ourselves. Have you ever wondered if one of your ancestors was a famous, important person? Perhaps your last name is Washington, and you've always fancied yourself as a distant relative of the heroic father of our country.

If you've shown a flair for painting or writing, maybe you've wondered if your talent is really in your genes, coming from an ancestor with a name like Da Vinci or Shakespeare. By climbing your family tree you may discover fascinating and inspiring information about your roots and even yourself.

Genealogy (jen-ee-ahl'-uh-jee) is the science or study of family lineage or ancestry. John Garland Pollard defined genealogy as "tracing yourself back to people better than you are." It is as old as the Bible, which serves as the first written example of family history. Although some people think genealogy is just a "dead" subject, family history is the most popular hobby today in America, ranking above even traditional favorites such as football and baseball! The first day that the enormous database of worldwide family records became available on www.familysearch.org it received over one million hits, more traffic than any other web site in history. Any pastime claiming to be more popular than baseball may sound almost un-American, yet family history is at the core of patriotism. A love of country and personal heritage leads to one of the most patriotic hobbies you could have: genealogy!

Alex Haley wrote, "Each discovered United States family history becomes a newly revealed small piece of American history. Stated simply: a nation's history is only the selective histories of all of its people. It is only through an unfolding of the people's histories that a nation's culture can be studied in its fullest meaning." (*Ethnic Genealogy: A Research Guide*, 1983)

As you begin the task of unraveling the mystery that is your origin, you will learn a great deal about the history of cultures and geography. This search for your roots will take you through time, from exotic places both on paper and in your imagination, and will give you a greater sense of just exactly how you fit into this giant web of people and places that we call the history of mankind. As you research your heritage, you will see the role you and your family play in the country where you now reside, often learning of traditions and sacrifices ancestors have made to bring you there. It becomes a spiritual experience to discover how we are all part of one great whole. A sense of belonging develops that provides an anchor for you as you try to find your place in a world that is whizzing by. This new great hobby of ours may take hold on more of you than you'd even like:

Cooking? Cleaning? I'd rather do Genealogy!
by Mel Oshins

They think that I should cook and clean, and be a model wife.
I tell them it's more interesting to study Grandpa's life.
They simply do not understand why I hate to go to bed....
I'd rather do two hundred years of research work instead.
Why waste the time we have on earth just snoring and asleep
When we can learn of ancestors that sailed upon the deep?
We have priests, Rabbis, lawmen, soldiers, more than just a few.
And yes, there are many scoundrels, and a bootlegger or two.
How can a person find this life an awful drudge or bore
When we can live the lives of all those folks who came before?
A hundred years from now, of course, no one will ever know
Whether I did laundry, but they'll see our Tree and glow...
'Cause their dear old granny left for them, for all posterity,
Not clean hankies and the like, but a finished family tree.
My home may be untidy, 'cause I've better things to do...
This old granny's pulling roots and branches out with glee,
Her clothes ain't hanging out to dry, she's hung up on The Tree!

Genealogy is not family group records, pedigree charts, microfilms, technical regulations or lengthy lists of "he begets." These are only some of the tools. Family history seeks to study one's own family members from birth through childhood, marriage, career, posterity, and on up to death. Each person's life is connected to those who came before, as well as to those who are yet to come.

There is a single thread that ties those heartstrings together. To study one's family is to study one's self. While facts such as names, locations, and dates are the skeleton of a genealogist's work, to flesh out a family's personal history is what makes the search rewarding. A part of our ancestors lives still, deep within us.

So why have so many millions of people become involved and even driven by an obsessive passion to research their family history? The reasons are as varied as the leaves on a tree. One reason may be the simplest: just because it's fun! Remember the joy of playing hide and seek as a child? Genealogy has a bit of that same mystery and intrigue. As you look for clues about your heritage, you get that same child-like thrill when you find that elusive ancestor who had been hiding. Digging for family roots also gives you that same sense of joy when you dug in the dirt as a child. It was fun to just feel the earth under your fingertips and crumble the dirt.

Searching for your ancestors is often dirty work, as you may often find yourself digging amongst dusty old books and archives. It really gets "earthy" when you take field trips to cemeteries! There's a human element of fun when you're researching people who really lived and not just searching for faceless names, dates and places. One girl's genealogy-obsessed mother had to chuckle when her young daughter named her dolls one day, "Jenny, Jennifer and Jenealogy."

So how could romping through cemeteries and turning pages in old, dog-eared books be fun, you ask? You many never understand it until you've tried it. If you're the kind of person who likes to "people-watch" at airports or other busy places because you think we humans are just so doggone entertaining, then you're going to love doing genealogy! Death is just part of the journey of the human experience. These statements on real death certificates demonstrate the humor even in death:

+ "Died. Nothing serious."
+ "Went to bed and woke up dead."
+ "Died. Don't know why—never had a fatal illness before!"
+ "Cause of death: an ax over the head. Precipitory cause: someone else's wife!"
+ "He died for want of another breath."

Others are attracted to recording their family lineage for academia's sake. Tracing lines of lineage and ancestry is as ancient as the history of man. Lineages were originally shared orally from generation to generation and later societies began to write them down. Tribal lineage was recorded by the House of Israel in the Bible, as well as by the Greeks, Romans and Chinese cultures. Lists of hereditary kings were compiled by the ancient Sumerians, Babylonians, Egyptians, Indians and Asians. In medieval Europe, landholders kept records of lineage to establish rights to land, property and rank. Attention to descent and rank was also demonstrated in coats of arms for many societies.

One of the original uses of genealogy was to prove that a person was descended from particular kings and queens in order to acquire certain benefits or level of status. Not surprisingly, until the 16th century, the science of genealogy was most often used by either rulers or upper class families. Extensive records began to be kept later, making it far easier for us ordinary citizens to trace our lineage. Today, anyone can research their history to find out if they meet qualifications for admittance into social organizations, such as the Sons of the American Revolution or even to find out if their heritage qualifies them for a certain college scholarship.

Still, others are intrigued by their genetic lineage, often as a result of questions such as why a red-headed daughter with freckles emerged in a family of all dark-haired boys. Are Great Aunt Althea's genes coming through or is that elusive milkman at work again?

Tracing a particular genetic composition can be extremely helpful for someone who needs to know what medical problems may be lurking or to understand how to avoid certain health tendencies in their family. Knowing Diabetes, Lupis, or high cholesterol, for example, run in your family can be a great motivator for improving healthy habits in younger generations.

So how could romping through cemeteries and turning pages in old, musty books be fun, you ask? When Tracey was a young college student, she explained it in these words:

Midnight Madness With Microfilms

When I was in college I would work hard to finish assigned projects and papers so I could "reward" myself with well-deserved time in the genealogy section of our campus library. After several hours of digging through microfilms, I found some records that revealed some families I had been searching for. The library lights were dimming and music was being played on the speakers to warn students that the library would be closing in 15 minutes. My pulse raced with the clock as I read quickly through the films. The music stopped and the main lights turned off, but I was still entranced by my find. I was seated behind a microfilm reader, which was fairly dark, so the dimming lights didn't threaten me. I glanced around from my hidden corner and didn't see anyone. I continued searching greedily for my treasure. At least 45 minutes later after recording details from my new discovery, I meandered out behind my sacred cove to the exit of the library. My evening would have been perfect, except for the security guard, who halted my escape and began to interrogate me, asking why I was still in the library. After trying to explain to him of my great genealogical discovery and the urgent need to complete the task, he rolled his eyes with intolerance and unlocked the doors for my exit. Trying to explain to someone about a precious genealogical find, who doesn't share the same obsession with genealogy, is like trying to explain the savor of salt to someone who has never tasted it!

Many genealogists have been found in a compulsive trance in front of a microfilm reader in their quest for finding familiar names or dates to document their family connections. The fire of this kind of passion is kindled by something deeper than a mere hobby for fun. For some, researching their family history is quite a spiritual quest when they read in Malachi 4:5, which offers a sweet promise, as well as a stern warning, "Behold, I will send you Elijah the prophet, before the coming of the great and dreadful day of the Lord; and he shall turn the heart of the fathers to the children, and the heart of the children to their fathers, lest I come and smite the earth with a curse."

The Church of Jesus Christ of Latter-day Saints has the world's largest collection of genealogy data, and freely shares it with anyone who is interested. Because of their belief in the eternal family unit they have gathered family history records of over 1.5 billion deceased people. To members of the Church, nothing is more important or rewarding than family. The Church has an impressive mission to acquire and preserve the records of mankind and help families find the links to their family chains.

Most religions proclaim some form of an afterlife and that, although our ancestors have preceded us in death, teach that we expect to see them again and live with them. The "veil" that separates the living family members from those who have passed on is often thin, and an unseen hand, perhaps from a loving ancestor watching on, seems to help guide the efforts of the researcher. It doesn't take long before the genealogist, amateur or professional, experiences serendipitous events that make one wonder who is really helping them. Perhaps it is the hand of God or even Elijah, as was prophesied to turn hearts of the children to their fathers, that aids us in our efforts to find one another and turn our hearts to one another.

What is it that keeps family history seekers going even after hours of tedious research? It is each small success of finding that special name or document to prove relationships. There is a pull, an urge and even a power that propels their quest. It is the spiritual element. It's as if they hear "whispers through the leaves" as they climb their family trees. The intuition to look in certain records or places seems to represent a thinning of the veil that separates live mortals from those who have only moved to another sphere. Perhaps our ancestors want to be found even more desperately than we want to find them. They, somehow, are allowed to whisper through the veil to help us connect the generations. In researching our family tree mysteries, our own ancestors often become the guides. It becomes a truly sacred experience, a powerful motivation for many genealogists.

One woman remarked, "This genealogy is more than just a hobby. Strange things happen to me all the time. Pages turn in the books that I am reading. I get these funny hunches which prove very successful. I hear voices in the night. And I often have dreams about my ancestors. It is as if genealogy effects both heaven and earth."

Another amateur genealogist of ten years explained, "I feel there is a spiritual connection versus 'coincidences' when working on one's family history. I feel that just about every 'coincidence' in life is, indeed, a spiritual experience."

It is our hope that this book will not only provide you with useful information in your genealogy journey, but also encouragement for when you hit those roadblocks or feel overwhelmed. This book contains a compilation of many stories that demonstrate the magical moments and experiences treasured by genealogists, both amateur and professional. The objective is to inspire, educate and uplift your weary eyes as you take a break from searching for your own ancestors. As in climbing real trees, family tree climbers need to stop and rest awhile to enjoy the view before ascending further. While you enjoy these true stories by fellow researchers, may you feel refreshed and full of hope to begin your climbing again. But be careful—that genealogy bug just might get you!

By the way, we wanted to make this book an adventure for you in itself. Because genealogists love a good hunt, we thought we'd create a fun one for you. On each page of this book is a small leaf. On a particular page, there is a leaf that is lighter than all the rest.

When you find the lighter leaf, log on to our website at www.climbingtrees.com and let us know on what page it is hidden. If you're right, then we'll send you a free gift! Hey, that alone was worth the price of this book, right? A mystery, a hunt, and then a prize. Can you handle this much fun?

And finally, in order to make this book a truly helpful tool, we're going to give you an assignment at the end of each chapter. Don't panic, it won't be difficult, but it will be something to help push you along the path of progress in your genealogy research. By the time you finish reading this book you will not only have gained some useful research tips and have felt the Spirit of Elijah tugging at your heart, but you will also have completed some specific tasks that you might have been putting aside for "some day." Happy heritage hunting!

CHAPTER ASSIGNMENT:

Write down why you want to research your family's roots. Why is it important to you? What will you do with the information when you find it? How will you share it with your family and the world?

_____

_____

_____

_____

_____

_____

_____

_____

CHAPTER 2

Measure The Tree Height

Finding out what's been done, gathering and organizing information

In any worthwhile endeavor, the hardest part is just getting started. Beginning to ascend a Giant Redwood, which reaches hundreds of feet above the ground, would be quite intimidating for anyone, yet by surveying the height and calculating small steps through lower branches, the monumental task becomes possible. Once started, how far you climb depends on you. Many books have already been written about how to begin genealogy and they all identify the most important starting point ... YOU!

Where To Begin

Begin by collecting any documents or photos you have about YOUR life. Start with certificates that document your birth, blessing, christening or confirmation. Add education records from preschool through college years, marriage certificate, professional designations and awards, as well as anything that documents your life story. Don't try to do this all in one day! It may take awhile to gather all of the things you have scattered in various places from the attic to the garage to your family Bible, wherever that is! Place them in some kind of safe organizer, such as a binder with sheet protectors or just a manila folder that groups them together temporarily. Then organize them chronologically. These items will also help you when writing your autobiography, a wonderful part of your genealogy! Who better to write your life's lessons, triumphs and joys than you? Everyone has a story to tell.

Most of us have piles of precious family photographs in boxes, waiting to be labeled, organized, put into scrapbooks, scanned into the computer, or put into frames. Don't let another year go by with those faces fading from both light and people's memories. You may need to get together with other relatives in order to identify and label the photos. Make a party of it or include it as a project at your next family reunion! Even if you don't have time to scrapbook or display them properly yet, make sure you get them out of old envelopes and shoeboxes and into archival quality plastic sleeves or acid-free photo boxes before they are lost forever. Make copies and share them with as many family members as possible. Copies of treasured photos make wonderful gifts for other family members. The recipients will certainly enjoy the gift, and each additional copy helps to ensure that they will not be lost forever in the event of fire or flood.

After you have collected everything available about yourself, begin to collect documents regarding your own parents, your spouse and your children. If you are overwhelmed by the accumulation of family history records that you have found stuffed in boxes and drawers, then set aside a regular time each week for organizing a little at a time. Take heart;

you will most likely find all sorts of new clues as you sort through the records and can later add the data and notes to your genealogy software program. (Add "genealogy software" to your new shopping list if you don't already have some!) Begin to create folders that extend your immediate family to include grandparents on both your maternal and paternal lines. Each parental couple who is written on your pedigree chart should then also have its own family group chart which shows all their children. And thus begins the great heritage treasure hunt as you collect photos, documents, certificates, and sources that tell the story of who you are and where you came from.

Be sure to cite your sources. "Where did I get this?" is an important question genealogists must consider all the time. Where you find facts about your ancestors can be very important, not only for your own further research, but for anyone else trying to follow what you have done. Consider everything in the attic or basement as a possible clue to learning more about your family history. Even old Christmas cards can be a source of information for finding long-lost relatives! Creating a paper trail of documentation also helps prevent useless duplication of someone else's time and ensures that you have the correct person.

The basic "Research Cycle" is to first identify what you know about your family. Second, decide what you want to learn about your family. Third, select the records that will give you the needed information. Fourth, obtain and search the record. Fifth, use and organize the new information to make connections. Last, but definitely not least, share your information with others! Don't forget to use that new information to strengthen your family relationships. And of course, begin the process again to learn even more!

Where To Write It All Down

The most basic forms for writing down your information about births, marriages, deaths and locations are the family group chart and pedigree chart. As you write in the names, dates and places for your direct line family you will be "measuring the tree height" in this exciting adventure of climbing family trees. You will easily see how much information you have, as well as the empty gaps of information where you can begin active research. One important reminder is the necessity to write down and document your findings and then to make sense of your information by using one of the family forms. Many a sad story is told of the excited genealogist who has accumulated reams of paper with valuable information from a trip to a genealogy library or cemetery only to add the treasured information to an already high stack of papers, without making any real connections to family. You can easily plug your information into charts used by software programs such as Personal Ancestral File or Family Tree Maker. You can even make family posters to give as Christmas gifts next year! Free charts can be found and downloaded from these websites:

www.familytreemagazine.com/forms/download.html

www.pbs.org//kbyu/ancestors/charts

www.ancestry.com/save/charts/ancchart.htm

www.genealogicalstudies.com

www.heritagequest.com/genealogy/help/html/pedigree.html

http://genealogy.about.com/

www.onepagegenealogy.com

www.wrhs.org/library/template.asp?id=196

www.misba/ch.orgpdfcharts/

Where To Learn More

Online classes that teach the basics of genealogy and the use of the helpful forms can be found at:

www.genealogy.com/university.html

www.rootsweb.com/

http://rwguide.rootsweb.com

www.generations.on.ca/family-history.htm

http://ce.byu.edu/is/site/catalog/pe.dhtm

www.myfamily.com/isapi.dll (Fee required)

www.ngsgenealogy.org/courses/course.cfm

www.genealogicalstudies.com

genealogy.about.com/od/free_classes/

www.kindredtrails.com/free_genealogy_stuff.html

www.bdgonline.com

www.aagg.org/03Resources/onlinecrs.html

Different forms employ various methods for writing down the vital information. It is strongly suggested you use black pen when writing notes by hand, as it is more effective when making copies and doesn't fade like pencil. Last names are more easily recognized when capitalized. Some forms prefer the surname written first, but you can decide which form you like the best. Just be sure to be consistent in all of your records. Writing complete dates rather than using the common short form helps to avoid confusion. For example, write 8 June 1872 instead of 6/8/72. It can be especially helpful since not all countries use the same short form. Consider these details the "leaves" on the family tree to help better identify what kind of tree you have.

How To Store All That Data

Storing all of this information in an organized and systematic method is essential in making effective steps up through the family tree. You can simply use binders with family group charts placed in alphabetical order like a phone book and position pedigree charts in ascending order starting with information about you on page 1. Or you may choose to invest in a computer software program which will organize all the data for you as you type in names on individual family group sheets and pedigrees. The prices vary along with technical support services and abilities to print charts. In alphabetical order, here are some of the most commonly used programs:

1. Ancestral Quest www.ancquest.com
2. Ancestry Family Tree www.aft.ancestry.com/
3. Brother's Keeper www.ourworld.compuserve.com/homepages/ Brothers_Keeper
4. Cumberland Family Tree www.cf-software.com
5. Ezitree www.ram.netau/users/ezitree
6. Family Historian www.family-historian.co.uk/
7. Family Matters www.matterware.com/
8. Family Reunion www.famware.com
9. Family Tree Legends www.familytreelegends.com/
10. Family Tree Maker www.familytreemaker.com
11. GEDitCOM www.geditcom.com/
12. Gene www.ics.uci.edu/~eppstein/gene
13. Genealogical Information Manager www.gimsoft.com/
14. Genius www.gensol.com.au/genius.htm
15. Geneatique www.cdip.com/geneatiq.htm

16. Heredis www.heredis.com
17. Heritage Family Tree   www.individualsoftware.com/new/consumer/details/fd2_details.htm
18. KinQuest www.orelle.com/Kinquest/kinquest.htm
19. Legacy Family Tree www.legacyfamilytree.com
20. Lifelines www.lifelines.sourceforge.net/
21. The Master Genealogist www.whollygenes.com
22. Oedipus II www.lamain.nl/oedipus.htm
23. Personal Ancestral File www.familysearch.org
24. Pocket Genealogist www.northernhillssoftware.com/mainframe.htm
25. Reunion www.leisterpro.com
26. RootsMagic www.rootsmagic.com

Grandma Climbed the Family Tree

by Jim Bates
Australia

There's been a change in Grandma, we've noticed it of late.
She's always reading history or jotting down some date.
She's tracing back the family, we'll all have pedigrees;
Grandma's got a hobby, she's climbing family trees.
Poor Grandpa does the cooking and now, or so he states,
He even has to wash the cups and dirty dinner plates.
Well Grandma can't be bothered, she's busy as a bee.
Compiling genealogy for the family tree.
She's got no time to baby-sit, the curtains are a fright,
No buttons left on Grandpa's shirts, the flower bed's a sight.
She's given up her Club work, the serials on TV,

The only thing she does nowadays is climb the family tree.
The mail is all for Grandma, it comes from near and far.
Last week she got the proof she needs to join the DAR.
A monumental project, to that we all agree,
A worthwhile avocation, to climb the family tree.
She wanders through the graveyard in search of date and name.
The rich, the poor, the in-between, all sleeping there the same.
She pauses now and then to rest, fanned by a gentle breeze,
That blows above the fathers of all our family trees.
Now some folk came from Scotland, and some from Galway Bay.
Some were French as pastry, some German all the way.
Some went on West to stake their claims, some stayed there by the
    sea,
Grandma hopes to find them all as she climbs the family tree.
There were pioneers and patriots mixed with our kith and kin,
Who blazed the paths of wilderness, and fought through thick and
    then.
But none more staunch than Grandma, whose eyes light up with
    glee;
Each time she finds a missing branch for the family tree.
Their skills were wide and varied, from carpenter to cook,
And alas, the records show was hopelessly a crook.
Blacksmith, farmer, weaver, Judge, some tutored for a fee;
Once lost in time, now all recorded, on the family tree.
To some it's just a hobby, to Grandma it's much more.
She learns the joys of heartaches of those who went before.
They loved, they lost, they laughed, they wept, and now for you
    and me;
They live again in spirit round the family tree.

At last she's nearly finished, and we are all exposed.
Life will be the same again, this we all suppose.
Grandma will cook and sew, serve crullers with our tea,
We'll have her back, just as before that wretched family tree.
Sad to relate, the Preacher called and visited for a spell,
We talked about the Gospel, and other things as well.
The heathen folk, the poor and then.. 'Twas fate it had to be,
Somehow the conversation turned to Grandma and the family
*   tree.*
We tried to change the subject, we talked of everything.
But then in Grandma's voice we heard that old familiar ring.
She told him all about the past, and soon 'twas plain to see;
The preacher too, was neatly snared by Grandma and the Family
*   Tree!*

("Crullers served with our tea" is believed to be of Dutch origin. Twisted
pieces of pastry fried in deep oil.)

Don't Leaf Anything Out

Filling out pedigree sheets and family group charts may seem quite tedious and even boring at times, except for the fact that as you write names, dates and places you begin to picture each person and family in your mind. The very act of writing down documents allows an often spiritual connection with each family.

Computer programs now make the data entry easier and also provide alarms or red flags if data doesn't seem logical. When entering twin births, for example, many genealogy programs will create an on-screen message, telling you the two births are not nine months apart. If you are certain the children are twins, then just smile and be grateful that you are smarter than the computer. There will be other times when you aren't! You might see children with the same name listed on a family group sheet and wonder what that story is.

Often when parents lost a baby to death they would name the next child with the same name in honor of the first child. Researchers may accidentally delete one of these children thinking it is a duplicate if they're not careful with details. Sibling sleuthing requires close attention to details.

Computer programs help you reconsider such information and begin to think critically about the dynamics of a family's life. When writing down many children for a family you may notice a large gap between children's births, which may lead to clues. Perhaps the family moved to another location and the family can be found on another census record in another county or state.

Looking at a family group record which shows several childhood deaths can pull on your heartstrings and make you feel closer to the parents who endured such loss. Taking time to look at dates and places gives you a glimpse back into time to very real people whose blood still flows through your veins. This is where "hearts are turned to their father's" (Malachi 4:5, 6).

Just as a blank space representing a missing name on a family group record is unsettling to you, it might be even more so to the very people who may help you fill in the gaps. Your ancestors want to be found! Those gaps on your pedigree charts can often be filled by the most unexpected sources, as Tracey explains in the following experience:

Best Boring Lecture I Was Forced to Attend

Like any college student knows, juggling classes with projects, tests, books, a hopeful social life and other demands is a constant battle for balance. After being diligent in my Nursing School responsibilities I would "reward" myself by going to the Genealogy Library on campus for a few hours at the end of each week to explore new families on my pedigree chart.

Every year my university would host a special Education Week, featuring various topics and speakers, but I never could justify going to any of the classes due to my own full study schedule. I tortured myself as I picked up one of the brochures that listed all of the interesting classes and guest speakers to be offered during that week. I knew I wouldn't be able to attend so why did I even pick up the pamphlet?

Then my eyes widened as I noticed one of the speakers had the same surname as a family I had been researching recently. Like someone with a new allergy who has a heightened awareness to his physical surroundings, a genealogist is more attuned to surnames he's working on. The speaker, Mr. Arrington, also came from the same location in North Carolina as my ancestors! I marked the lecture time and location on my calendar and during the next week crossed it off and back on several times as I debated the reality of my restricted time.

At the very hour of Mr. Arrington's lecture I stood at the door, wrestling with myself to either go in or attend the required class I was supposed to be in for my student work. It was as if someone unseen pushed me through the door, and so I reluctantly sat down in the back row. The lecture itself was a bit boring and I struggled to remain seated, but I was driven to stay by my unanswered questions. Was this man was a distant relative of mine? If so, could he help me find missing links in my Arrington family line?

After his presentation, a long line began to form quickly of eager audience members wanting to shake his hand and discuss more ideas. I knew I would have wasted my time if I didn't get in that line and ask him about his family heritage, but the line now represented another half hour of waiting. Again, I felt something move my legs to the line even though I murmured in my mind about how much time I would be wasting. Would he be offended by my asking him a personal question? Would he be bothered that my questions were off the topic of his presentation?

Finally, my turn came and I sheepishly stammered my query. He said the names I was relating didn't sound familiar, then casually gave me his card and told me to write him with the details. That afternoon I wrote the specifics of my Arrington family line and sent the letter with return postage and a prayer. Weeks passed and I received nothing. What a waste. Like a thirsty desert traveler who greedily drinks rationed water, I would rush to my mail box every day, hoping for any genealogy correspondence.

Finally, after a very long time, I received a large manila envelope from Mr. Arrington! His first sentence was, "By golly, we're related!" He then outlined our connection and detailed more information about our shared great grandparents, burial sites and family group sheets. The information he presented allowed me to extend my Arrington family line back five generations with hundreds of cousins!

Because of names and connections made through him we discovered that an Arrington man working in my mother's office was also a distant cousin! Suddenly, there was an instant bond *because of shared heritage. People who were once strangers became family in an instant. I still treasure that letter, as it represents to me how persistent my Arrington ancestors were in getting me to the lecture that day. I believe there were more people sitting in the lecture hall that day than he could see!*

CHAPTER ASSIGNMENT:

Choose a family line that you would like to begin to work on. Write down the name of one relative that you can begin to research this week. What will you do with that informaion?

_____

_____

_____

_____

_____

_____

_____

_____

_____

_____

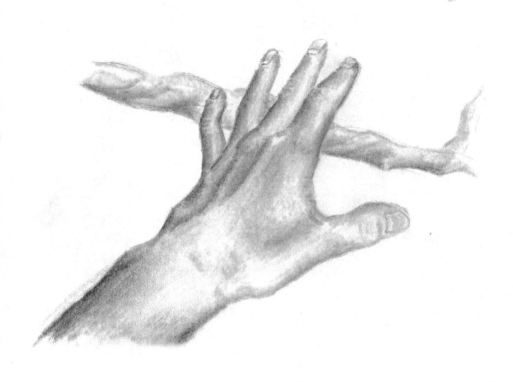

CHAPTER 3

Grab On To A Branch

Choosing a family line for research and interviewing relatives

This chapter, entitled "Grab On To A Branch" means just that—pick a name and start! Start somewhere, anywhere! Just do it! There is plenty of help available, both here on earth and in heaven. You just have to do your part and get started! Don't worry that you don't have all of the information you need. That's when the fun research begins! This chapter is filled with stories about regular people who were looking for just one ancestor and ended up finding so much more. There is an old Hebrew proverb that says "There must be a stirring below before there is a stirring above."

Now is the time to get in touch with those relatives you've been meaning to contact! Start with the oldest relatives first. Some of them may have information about the family that can't be found anywhere else, and let's face it, they won't be around forever to ask. When possible, try to video or tape record your interview. Even the most detailed notes will never be able to describe your Great Aunt Paula's laughter or capture

Grandpa Jack's baby blue eyes. Remember to take your camera too!

It's helpful to bring a written list of questions you want to ask. It will keep your interview on task and provide specific conversation starters for the shy interviewee. What makes family history fascinating are not the names and dates, but the colorful stories and details of your ancestors' lives.

Be sensitive to your older relatives' time and health. Asking all of the questions below would surely tire them out! An ancient proverb, probably written by a genealogist counsels, "The mind can absorb only what the seat can endure." Sometimes when you interview living relatives you'll get conflicting information or data that doesn't add up. Don't worry! Keep taking notes and asking those questions. Sooner or later you'll find one piece of information that will make it all fit together!

When you don't have the luxury of interviewing a relative in person, phone calls and letters can still be very effective. A two-page letter is easier to read and respond to than a 20-page one! Shorter phone calls or letters can hold your interviewee's attention much better, so don't try to get a lifetime's worth of information out of just one conversation. If you're using the pen and paper as your interview method, include a cover letter. For an example see: www.familytreemaker.com/00000059. html. For more ideas on interview questions, hints and protocol check out the Capturing the Past website at www.byubroadcasting.org/capturingpast/.

It's often helpful to divide a lifetime into segments of time. If you're writing your own autobiography or someone else's biography you could work on a few questions or time frames each week or month. Writing life segments is less intimidating than thinking you have to write an entire lifetime in one sitting.

Here are a few suggestions for good interview questions to get you started:

Interview Question Ideas

CHILDHOOD AND YOUTH

+ Please share one memory of your mother.
+ Please share one memory of your father.
+ Please share one memory of each brother.
+ Please share one memory of each sister.
+ Please share one memory of your mother's parents or aunts, uncles or cousins.
+ Please share one memory of your father's parents or aunts, uncles or cousins.
+ Where was the location of your house? Is it still standing? What did it look like?
+ Do you remember your grandparent's houses? Where were they? Are they still standing? What did they look like? Do you have any pictures?
+ What kind of mischief did you get into as a child? How strict were your parents?
+ What chores were assigned to you to do? Did you receive any spending money? If so, what did you do with it?
+ Did you have any nicknames?

SCHOOL DAYS

- What are your most vivid memories of your childhood?
- What were your dreams and aspirations?
- What did you want to be when you grew up?
- Where did you attend school? How far was it from your home? How did you get there?
- What subjects did you like best? Least?
- Who were your best friends in school? Do you keep in touch?
- What memories stand out about your school days?
- What did you do during the summer when you were not in school?
- Did you ever visit and spend the night with friends or relatives?
- What were your favorite toys? Games?
- What was your favorite song? TV show? Movie?
- Were there any unusual events in your childhood? (moving, storms, floods, fires, world events, etc.)
- What was the highest level of education you received?

ADOLESCENCE

- When did you start dating? What rules were imposed at your house regarding dating?
- How late you could stay out and where you could go? Did you have a chaperone?
- When you went on a date what did you do?
- What were the rules in your house regarding the following: playing cards, going to movies, dancing, eating with the adults, girls wearing slacks to school, and "proper manners."

- What neighborhood gatherings do you recall?
- What were your favorite subjects in school?
- Who were your best friends?
- What were the fashions of your day?

RELIGION

- Did you attend a church? Where was the church? What was it like?
- Were there any special religious events in your life?
- Did you have a favorite scripture verse? Hymn? Song?
- Do you recall an experience with death as a child or teenager?
- Have you become more or less religious over the years?
- What was your most spiritual experience?
- Were you baptized?

SOCIAL LIFE

- Did you participate in any type of recreation or athletics?
- Did you or any of your family sing or play musical instruments?
- Did you like to read? What were your favorite books as a child? As an adult?
- Did you learn a hobby or craft as a child or teenager? Did you continue to use it as an adult?
- Were you involved in any community affiliations or clubs?
- What was your first job? Where? What did you do? How much did you earn?
- Have you kept in touch with any friends from when you were growing up?
- Did you win any awards or contests?

DATING AND MARRIAGE

- Did you date a lot before you got married?
- How did you meet your spouse?
- What attracted you most to your spouse?
- Tell me about your courtship, proposal, and engagement.
- When and where did you get married? Describe the wedding day.
- What makes a successful marriage?
- Tell me about your first kiss.

PARENTHOOD AND FAMILY LIFE

- How did you decide what to name each child?
- What stands out about each of your children as a small child, adolescent, and teenager?
- What houses have you lived during your marriage? Where? Describe them.
- What jobs did you have to support your family?
- What trips have you taken as a family? Which have you enjoyed the most? Least?
- What holiday traditions did your family share? (Eating certain foods, meeting in certain places, gifts, events, etc.)
- Do you enjoy participating in music, art, gardening, needlework, sewing, carpentry, mechanics, etc.? Which members of the family did these activities?
- What was your first car? How much did it cost?
- Name other cars you had over the years. Which was your favorite?

YOUR LEGACY

- ✦ What inventions have changed your lifestyle? How?
- ✦ What do you consider your special talents or abilities?
- ✦ Are there any "words of wisdom" you would like to pass down to future generations?
- ✦ What was your most memorable Christmas or other holiday?
- ✦ What were some of your greatest challenges in life?
- ✦ What were some of your greatest accomplishments in life?
- ✦ Were there any wars in your lifetime that affected you and your family?
- ✦ Were there any remarkable natural phenomena?
- ✦ Who were the people that most touched your life? Why?
- ✦ What was your health like throughout your life?
- ✦ Describe yourself physically.
- ✦ What things made you happiest in your life?
- ✦ What things made you most sad in your life?
- ✦ What were your activities and hobbies that inspired your passion in life?
- ✦ If you had to live your life all over again, what would you do differently?
- ✦ What do you hope your legacy will be?

Who Are You?

While you interview your relatives you'll probably hear some new names mentioned, long-lost cousins who fit into your family tree. An easy description for all of those miscellaneous relatives is "cousin" but there's actually a way to figure out the familial relationship.

The editors of www.genealogy.com easily describe it the following way:

If someone walked up to you and said "Howdy, I'm your third cousin, twice removed," would you have any idea what they meant? We all have a good understanding of basic relationship words such as "mother," "father," "aunt," "uncle," "brother," and "sister." What about the relationship terms that we don't use in everyday speech? Terms like "second cousin" and "first cousin, once removed"? We don't tend to speak about our relationships in such exact terms. "Cousin" seems good enough when you are introducing one person to another, but how, exactly, is Cousin Jodie related to you? Sometimes, especially when working on your family history, it's handy to know how to describe your family relationships more precisely.

There are even all kinds of grids and relationship maps you can find on the Internet that diagram your family. There is something about a blood relation that instantly bonds us emotionally. The definitions below should help you out:

Cousin (a.k.a. first cousin)

Your first cousins are the people in your family who have two of the same grandparents as you. In other words, they are the children of your aunts and uncles.

Second Cousin

Your second cousins are the people in your family who have the same great-grandparents as you, but not the same grandparents.

Third, Fourth, and Fifth Cousins

Your third cousins have the same great-great-grandparents, fourth cousins have the same great-great-great-grandparents, and so on.

Removed

When the word "removed" is used to describe a relationship, it indicates that the two people are from different generations. You and your first cousins are in the same generation (two generations younger than your grandparents), so the word "removed" is not used to describe your relationship.

The words "once removed" mean that there is a difference of one generation. For example, your mother's first cousin is your first cousin, once removed. This is because your mother's first cousin is one generation younger than your grandparents and you are two generations younger than your grandparents. This one-generation difference equals "once removed."

Twice removed means that there is a two-generation difference. You are two generations younger than a first cousin of your grandmother, so you and your grandmother's first cousin are first cousins, twice removed.

The Family Puzzle

Cheryl Kay Richman Lippard

I began my family history research about 25 years ago. I took a course in a church Sunday School class and got bitten by the Genealogy Bug. I was very successful in finding information on my ancestors, as I grew up in the same area where all my great-

grandparents on my mother's pedigree had lived right before they died. I started at the county level and found the records for births, deaths, and marriages of many of my German ancestors. What made this so fantastic was that I was allowed into the record keeping area and was able to look at the original logs of the county. The funniest story is about my German great grandfather, Ferdinand Knopp, who went to the market and purchased a strange but beautiful yellow fruit which he had never seen before. He took his purchase home and bit into it, only to find it very bitter and tough. In disgust he threw the whole bunch of bananas away. He did not know that they needed to be peeled first!

I remember the first time I found deceased ancestors in a cemetery. How thrilling it was to see hard evidence that they had really existed! I was fortunate to receive family Bibles with birth, marriage and death information.

A family historian heard that I was digging into my roots and she sent me her records of the history of the Hackett family, which covered a span of 200 years! Yes, it was hearsay, but in time I have been able to document most of her findings with hard evidence. The clues keep coming in as I continue to do my family history research.

I found relatives who were neighbors of the Abraham Lincoln family, as well as of an indentured servant from Ireland, who held the reins of Daniel Boone's horse as he fought Indians. I have several Revolutionary War soldiers in my family tree, as well as Civil War soldiers. Another relative, Ninian Beall, was reported to have started the Presbyterian Church in the United States.

I am now doing research in most every state of the Eastern and Midwest sections of the United States, as well as in Germany,

England, France, Scotland, Wales, and Ireland. The list keeps growing with each new discovery.

I am not claiming any fame, but it really makes history come alive for me to know that some of my people were a part of this great nation's history. We had British sympathizers, German immigrants, Irish immigrants, Lords, Ladies, and Knights in our ancestral line as well as farmers, blacksmiths, and ministers, all hard-working people. I have found their religious and political beliefs, their physical descriptions, have obtained their signatures, and so many wonderful things to cherish. I continue to search for the records of my relatives and am currently researching the early 1800s in Germany.

I can trace my family back to England to the 1200s. In some lines I am still trying to find when my ancestors immigrated to the United States. If we weren't on the Mayflower, we certainly were right behind it!

I can only imagine the life that my early ancestors led. I would love to have a time machine to travel back to visit and see all that they experienced. I know they made sacrifices for future generations and I am so thankful for this.

I love finding the missing pieces and hope to some day make a difference in the lives of my own descendants. I hope my records will bring light to their life about their ancestors. Yes, it is one huge puzzle, but certainly worth solving and putting together.

There are wonderful discoveries awaiting you, but be sure to cover those basic first steps. We certainly hope you have better success than the author of the following humorous poem:

Am I Really Me?

Author Unknown

I started out calmly, tracing my tree,
To find, if I could, the makings of me.
And all that I had was Great Grandfather's name,
Not knowing his wife's, nor from whence they both came.
I chased him across a long line of states
And came up with pages and pages of dates.
When all put together, it made me forlorn,
Proved poor Great Grandpa had never been born.
One day I was sure the truth I had found,
Determined to turn this whole thing upside down.
I looked up the record of one Uncle John,
Then found the old man was younger than his son.
But then when my hopes were growing quite dim,
I came across records that must have been him.
The facts I collected - they made me quite sad,
Dear old Great grandfather was never a dad.
I think someone surely is pulling my leg,
I'm not at all sure I'm not hatched from an egg.
After hundreds of dollars I've spent on my tree
I can't help but wonder if I'm really me.

CHAPTER ASSIGNMENT:

Who is your oldest living relative on your paternal side of the family? Who is the oldest on your maternal side? If possible, make arrangements to interview them in person. If they live simply too far, recruit help from a relative that lives closer who could film them in person, or write them letters weekly or monthly with selected questions that you want them to answer. How could you honor the patriarch and matriarch of your family this year?

_____

_____

_____

_____

_____

_____

_____

CHAPTER 4

Get A Leg Up

Available resources

Once you get a leg up on that family tree you may find yourself in unfamiliar territory, surrounded by a strange, new language. What exactly is the IGI or a GEDCOM file? Genealogists would make great game show contestants because they learn so much about a wide variety of topics from real estate to military to law and religion and more! Although this is certainly not an exhaustive genealogical glossary, here are some of the most common terms you will see as you research your family history:

Abstract   Abbreviated transcription of a document that includes the date of the record, every name appearing therein, the relationship of each person, their description, and if they signed with their signature or a mark.

Ahnentafel   A chart that tabulates the ancestry of one individual by generation in text rather than in pedigree chart format.

Ancestor	Any relative who lived before you.
b.	This is an abbreviation for BORN (example: b. 1740)
bef.	Abbreviation for BEFORE.
Bp or Bpt	Abbreviation for BAPTIZED.
Bro	Abbreviation for BROTHER.
Bu or Bur	Abbreviation for BURIED.
C or Ca	Abbreviation for CIRCA, which means about or around a certain date (example: Cooper Thomas Boice was born ca 1988)
Census	A listing of (supposedly) every person living in a country. The first U.S. Census was in 1790. Until 1850 only the head of household was listed; later other relatives were included, along with occupations, ages, and education. Don't even think about looking for the 1890 Census because it was destroyed in a fire. Most states also have census records.
Characteristics	Actions, attitudes and physical traits of a particular family.
Chr	Abbreviation for CHRISTENED. When a birth date or baptismal record isn't found then the Christened record can be used as acceptable documentation.
Christian Name	The "first" and sometimes "middle" name given to a child at birth.

Coat of Arms	A symbol showing the traits of a specific family, usually given to royalty. The artwork was often displayed on fabric, rugs, wall hangings, and crests.
Collateral	Family members who are not in your direct lines (cousins, aunts, in-laws, etc.)
Country of Origin	The country from which your earliest emigrant ancestor came.
D or Dau	Abbreviation for DAUGHTER.
Dec'd	Abbreviation for DECEASED, meaning someone who has died.
Descendant	Your own children and those who follow in your family line; anyone to whom you are an ancestor.
Deed	Document transferring ownership and title of land or other property.
Direct Line	The ancestor to whom you are most closely related and can trace "vertically" on a pedigree chart, such as a father, mother, grandfather, grandmother, etc.
Div	Abbreviation for DIVORCED.
Documentation	Written proof of any genealogical fact (certificates of birth, death, marriage, etc.)
Dowager	Widow holding property or a title from her deceased husband.
Emancipated	Freed from slavery or parents' control, of legal age.

Emigration   When an individual leaves his home country to live in another country.

Et al   "And Others."

Et ux   "And Wife."

Exec   Abbreviation for EXECUTOR, one who executes a will or carries out the directions in other legal documents upon someone's death. Executrix is a female appointed by a testator to perform the above tasks.

Family Group Sheet   A paper that contains information on one specific family, listing the mother, father and children.

Family History Center   A free genealogy library located in your local Church of Jesus Christ of Latter-day Saints. Patrons can use computers, books, microfiche, and film, as well as request information to be transferred from the Church's extensive library in Salt Lake City, Utah.

Feme or feme sole   Unmarried woman or a married woman with property independent of her husband.

FR   Abbreviation for FAMILY REGISTER.

Gdn or Grdn   Abbreviation for GUARDIAN, a person lawfully appointed to care for another person.

GEDCOM   (Genealogical Data Communications) A file format that allows different genealogical software programs to share data with each other, developed by the Church of Jesus Christ of Latter-day Saints, to help families exchange helpful information with one another.

Genealogy   The study of a person's family, its origins, and the progression from one generation to the next.

Genetic Traits Similar health patterns that flow through a family.

Heir   Person who succeeds, by the rules of law, to an estate upon the death of an ancestor.

Heritage   The characteristics, traits, and traditions of a family passed from one generation to the next.

Homestead   Property given to early settlers after they had lived on the land for a specified amount of time.

Husb   Abbreviation for HUSBAND.

IGI   (International Genealogical Index) An index of 250 million names created by the Church of Jesus Christ of Latter-day Saints. These were submitted to the Church or were extracted from records. They include records for baptisms, marriages, births and burials.

Immigration   The movement of people from one foreign country to another. A person involved in this is called an "emigrant."

Index   An alphabetical list of names that were taken from a particular set of records.

Indirect Line A family to whom you are related, but which branches off your direct line.

Inf	Abbreviation for INFANTRY.
Intestate	Used to denote a person who died without leaving a will.
Issue	Children, descendants, offspring.
Knave	Servant boy.
Knt	Abbreviation for KNIGHT.
Land records	Proof that a piece of land is owned by a particular individual.
Liber	Book of public records.
Lineage	The connection between a common family; tracing your family line to a particular ancestor.
Link	The joining of two separate family lines, as through marriage. Also an Internet hyperlink that connects to a certain web site.
Liv	Abbreviation for LIVING.
Loco parentis	In place of the parent or parents.
M or Md.	Abbreviation for MARRIED.
Major	A person who has reached legal age.
Migration	The movement of a family or group of people from one part of the country to another.
Mil	Abbreviation for MILITARY.
National Archives	This is the largest repository of government

genealogical materials in the United States, located in Washington D.C. Many states also have a portion of these records in their capital city.

Naturalization The act of becoming a citizen of a new country after immigration.

Natus   Born.

N.d.   Abbreviation for NO DATE.

Nunc   Abbreviation for NUNCAPATIVE WILL; an oral will dictated by the Testator before a sufficient number of witnesses and afterwards put into writing after the person dies.

Ob   Abbreviation for OBIT, deceased.

Octoroon   Child of a quadroon, a person having one-eighth black ancestry.

Old Dominion Virginia.

OS   Abbreviation for OLD STYLE CALENDAR; the Julian calendar used before the Gregorian calendar.

Oral History   Facts and stories spoken from one generation to another and passed on as a form of record keeping.

Passenger Lists   A roster of people who traveled from a foreign country on ships or trains to another location.

Pedigree   A genealogical form that usually shows five generations of a family.

Pension   Money paid to someone after they reach retirement age.

Posthumous   A child born after the death of the father.

Primary Line   The descendency through a person's father or mother.

Primary Source   A resource which can be documented and proven, such as church records, that contain a birth certificate or marriage license.

Private (Closed) Records   These are records not available to the general public, such as adoption and juvenile files.

Probate   Legal process used to determine the validity of a will; the passage of material wealth through the court system from an individual to heirs.

Progeniture   A direct ancestor.

Public Records   Records that are available to the general public, such as birth, marriage, death, tax and land records.

Q.V.   Abbreviation for Quod Vide; directs the reader to look in another part of the book for more information.

R.C.   Abbreviation for ROMAN CATHOLIC.

Relict or Relicata   Widow (Relictus is a widower.)

Ret   Abbreviation for RETIRED.

s.   Abbreviation for SON.

s. & h.   Abbreviation for Son & Heir.

S.A.S.E.   Abbreviation for SELF ADDRESSED STAMPED ENVELOPE, used as a courtesy to help pay for postage when requesting that someone send you information.

Secondary Line   The family line that follows a grandmother or great-grandmother.

Secondary Source   Records that may or may not be accurate, such as newspapers, journals, or certain books.

Serv.   Abbreviation for SERVANT.

Sic   Latin term signifying a copy reads exactly as the original; indicates a possible mistake in the original such as a spelling error.

S/O   Abbreviation for SOCIETY.

Social Security Death Index   An index of Social Security death records for United States citizens.

Soundex   An indexing system listed by phonetic spelling. This can be especially helpful when you aren't certain of how a name is spelled or as surnames evolve over the years.

St.   Abbreviation for STREET or SAINT. You'll need to figure that out based on context!

Surname   The "family" or "last" name of a group of related individuals.

T.	Abbreviation for TOWNSHIP; a tract of land usually 36 square miles.
Terr	Abbreviation for Territory.
Testate	Died leaving a valid will. (Testator = a man, and Testatrix = woman)
Unk	Abbreviation for UNKNOWN. (A genealogist's worst nightmare.)
Unm	Abbreviation for UNMARRIED.
Vital Records	Birth, marriage and death records.
Warranty Deed	A document that guarantees a clear property title from the seller to the buyer.
Yeoman	A farmer; a freeholder who works a small estate; the rank below gentleman. Believe it or not, you'll actually see this often as you look at documents!

One of the challenges of doing family history research is knowing where to look for the information you need! Someone once said, "Research is what you're doing when you don't know what you're doing!" Start with the information you have and think logically. If you're missing a certain piece of information then ask yourself "What document would show this data?" Some of the usual resources are legal certificates that show birth, death, and marriage. Be sure to check out wills, tombstones, census records, military documents, immigration lists, naturalization records, and real estate deeds.

When you think you've looked everywhere and still come up empty handed, don't forget to look on the Internet where you can find bulletin boards, the IGI, surname groups, and all kinds of new friends who are probably hunting for the same information! Just open your mouth and start talking (or typing) and before you know it someone will point you to that elusive document you were searching for. By the way, if you don't have a computer or Internet access, get them! There is so much research you can do at home in your slippers! Chapter 15 includes pages of web sites where you spend hours of sleuthing fun!

This is the best time in the history of the world for a genealogist to be alive, because of our access to literally millions of records and documents that were previously inaccessible to our forefathers. Dozens of books have been written about researching genealogy on the Internet. There are over 250,000 references to the word "genealogy" on the Internet! Surf the web with caution, however, as some sources are less trustworthy than others. Traditional methods of interviewing family members and taking field trips to cemeteries and courthouses are still priceless.

A primary source is a document or photo that was created at the time of an event with eye witnesses. An example would be certificates for birth, marriage and death, wills, and often family Bibles. Secondary sources are documents created after the event and not by an eye witness. Although a birth or death are often not witnessed by the person recording the certificate, they are still considered primary sources. Tertiary sources are more distant references such as biographies or indexes and encyclopedias of people. For more information on a comparison of primary, secondary and tertiary sources, check out the

Historian's Sources home page at the Library of Congress at http://www.lcweb2.loc.gov/ammen/ and http://www.library.uncwil.edu/is/infocycle.htm.

Vital records are among the most used primary sources, which include birth, marriage, divorce and death records. They are usually maintained by the county or parish where they originated and can be found among the governmental records of each state. Each state has varying laws regarding the release of records that can be viewed and they will let patrons know how to receive copies and what the fee may be. You can see what is available for each state in the United States at the Vital Records Information site http://www.vitalrec.com.

CENSUS RECORDS

The next most commonly used source for finding information about deceased people in the United States is through Census Records. Ever since 1790, a census of the population was conducted every ten years by an enumerator who counted people and families through towns and cities. It became a snapshot view of each family through time. Census records vary according to the amount of information they contain. The earliest census records often recorded only the name of the head of household, while later census records reported age, country of birth, literacy and field of work.

Census records are still recorded today, but because of rights of privacy and confidentiality, a 72-year hold is placed on viewing current records. You can presently view census records from 1790-1930. Sadly, the 1890 Census was largely destroyed by a fire in the U.S. Commerce building in 1921. Tracking families can be interesting and sometimes very challenging if they moved a lot.

A microfilmed index system, the American Soundex, can help you find the census record for surnames you are looking for. It's a clever system that breaks down all last names to several letters and then catalogs their location. For more information on the Soundex see: http://www. resources.rootsweb.com/cgi-bin/soundexconverter.

Many other countries have taken census reports throughout history including Australia, Austria, Canada, Denmark, Germany, Ireland, Italy, Norway and the United Kingdom. Records abound for these countries too and can be found using "census" as a keyword on many search engines.

After checking vital statistics records and census records, the next most popular resource for active research is land records. Historically, land ownership was the measurement of someone's success. Land deeds and records can often tell you a lot of information about the family who purchased the property. Land records are especially helpful when trying to track families in the United States before the 1790 census report. Again, most land records are held in the local county where they were created. Textbooks and reference materials are as expansive as the land being tracked. For more information on the Internet check out http://www.glorecords.blm.gov . For the Bureau of Land Management and the National Archives go to www.archieves.gov/research_room/ federal_records_guide/bureau_of_land_managment/

The following are some of the more well-known and reputable references on the Internet to help you with your research:

Cyndi will be your new best friend. That is, www.cyndislist.com where you'll find over 242,150 links to more genealogy web sites.

Providing the largest collection of genealogical records in the world, the Church of Jesus Christ of Latter-day Saints generously offers free access to anyone at www.familysearch.org

Can't find that map you need? Go to http://www.rootsweb.com/ ~usgenweb/maps/ for digital maps of the United States, including state and county maps, as well as Indian land cessions to the United States Treaty maps.

Do you wish you had some information about your ancestor who served in the Civil War? Check out http://www.rootsweb.com/ %7Eusgenweb/pensions/ to see actual transcriptions of pension related materials for all wars prior to 1900.

If you had an ancestor who served his country in the American Revolution, the Indian Wars, the Mexican War, the Civil War, or the Spanish-American War, he might have received a government pension. If your ancestor didn't apply, perhaps his parents, his widow or any dependent children and parents may have applied for one. Check out http://www.archives.gov/research_room/genealogy/research_topics/ military.html/

For a listing of sources for the records of various religions go to http://www.cyndislist.com/topical.htm

Here's a great web site resource where you could sign up for mailing lists to learn more about bygone towns, medieval times, orphan trains, families with Black-Dutch ancestry, witch trials worldwide, refugees, and a lot more: http://www.rootsweb.com/~jfuller/gen_mail_general. html

Courthouse records often are a goldmine of family nuggets and contain land deeds, census records, vital records, wills, probate records, tax records, military records and even clues to unlawful conduct by a mischievous ancestor. Calling ahead or writing the courthouse is a wise use of time as many records are safeguarded off site or have actually been destroyed. Of course the exact record you will be searching for will inevitably be in the one file lost to "the flood."

Often it is easy for a busy and underpaid clerk to say the document doesn't exist, which may make your personal visit more helpful. While visiting the local courthouse where your ancestor lived, you may also find it worthwhile to visit the local library. Public and private libraries have city directories and some historical information such as past newspapers and maps. For a list of online library catalogs check out the Library Index home page at www.libdex.com/.

Another resource for sleuthing is a historical society. Local societies will often have historical maps, histories, biographies and tips for researching that particular area. You may even find it valuable to join a historical or genealogical society in a location where your ancestors lived due to the common sharing of information among members. Historical societies are listed at www.dir.yahoo.com/arts/humanities/history/organizations/historical_societies/.

To find a genealogical society in the United States, the Federation of Genealogical Society Hall lists them on their site at: http://www.familyhistory.com/societyhall/main.asp.

There are many genealogy classes offered on the Internet, as well as courses taught by "real" people in your own community where you can get a great introduction to the wide variety of resources out there. If you're lucky enough to have a Family History Center in your community you can receive free help and hands-on training within minutes. Family History Centers are located inside the buildings of the Church of Jesus

Christ of Latter-day Saints and are available to anyone. Over two million rolls of microfilm, 400,000 books and millions of records on microfiche are available to the general public. To find a Family History Center in your area look up: http://www.familysearch.org/eng/Library/FHC/frameset_fhc.asp

Today, maneuvering around the World Wide Web is easier than ever. In our analogy of climbing family trees, trying to find data on the Internet used to be more like a trip to the jungle, with so many intertwined branches that made it difficult to see where one begins and one ends. As search engines become more refined, climbing family trees on the Internet is faster because there are more catalogs of different "trees" and the trees themselves are better pruned and organized.

Personal genealogy sites and one-name study sites can help you pinpoint your family surname and ancestors. The Guild of One-Name Studies is an online organization of over 7,000 registered sites that focuses on one particular surname. Check out www.one-name.org. Family associations and organizations also focus on one surname and are often organized with a body of officers and events, which is very helpful. You can share family information through e-mail or letters, or even attend a real family reunion with strangers who share a chromosome or two.

Your public library may even have a special section or floor dedicated just to genealogy and, if you're lucky enough to find a bored librarian, you can get a quick education on what books are available and what kinds of information may be found within them. Many capital cities host buildings where State or National Archives are kept. Helpful employees can point you in the right direction and get your feet wet in a sea of useful data. Don't be embarrassed to ask questions; inevitably, the person behind the desk will be a long lost relative or know where you can find one! If you want to see miracles, just do your genealogy!

When Wrong Tombstones are Right

by Edna Recine
Midlothian, Illinois

My daughter asked me if we could go visit the grave of my mother. My mother passed away during my birth so I never knew her. My father never spoke of her. Perhaps the pain was too great. He told me nothing about her family, but I did know where she was buried. Other people told me a little bit about her, but it wasn't much. I didn't even know her mother's name. I knew her mother had died during a child birth also. I knew my mom had an aunt whom I had met when I was very young, but I didn't remember her.

The day we went to the cemetery to visit my mother's grave, I told my daughter we should look for her aunt's grave also. We went into the office at the cemetery and got the grave lot number and directions to the parts of the cemetery where they were buried. We stopped at my mother's grave first. Then we drove to the area on the map that marked where her aunt was buried. My daughter walked down one side of the rows of tombstones and I walked facing the other row of tombstones.

We couldn't find my aunt's grave, and had walked all the way to the next road, when a cemetery worker asked us what we were looking for. He looked at the map, looked up and asked, "Is that your red car parked down there?" When I told him it was he said we had walked right past the grave, and that he would show us where it was. As we were walking back to the site, for some reason, I felt compelled to stop in the middle of the row of tombstones and read one particular tombstone. The name at the top of the large stone did not mean anything to me, but as my eyes scrolled down, I read a woman's name and date of death, a baby's name and date of death, and a man's name and date of death. The man's surname happened to be the same as the name of the aunt whose grave we were seeking. I wondered and kept walking.

After we went to find my aunt's grave, I told my daughter about the stone I had seen in the middle of the row. We went back and my daughter wrote down all the names and important dates. The next day she then went to the library in downtown Chicago and went through the microfilmed newspapers surrounding the dates of the deaths on the tombstone. What she found was amazing. The woman was my mother's mother! She had divorced my mother's father and had remarried (thus a different last name on the tombstone). The baby would have been my mother's sister. The man was my mother's uncle, who was crushed in a train accident when he was just 18 years of age.

I would have never found these deceased relatives if not for the compelling feeling I had that day that made me stop in my tracks and read that particular tombstone. I like to believe that my mother somehow sent me the feeling from above.

Bless Those Cursed Names

by Clyde Rice

I had been searching for years for my 3rd great grandfather. The first "whisper" I heard was while I was perusing the Internet for any possible clues one day. A couple of folks told me that this 2nd great grandfather's father's name was Ephraim. Whoa, alarm bells rang inside my head! That is the name that my dad always called those little Jersey bull calves! Now, I don't know if Dad even knew he had a 2nd great grandfather by the name of Ephraim. Maybe he had always heard an old family saying like, "As stubborn and bullheaded as Old Ephraim!"

With just that little clue, I have traced Ephraim and his family from Catskill, New York in 1790, right through Tioga County in Pennsylvania, with a stop in between at Chenango, Broome County in New York in 1825. This connection to the previous surname has helped me find six more generations! My Ephraim had just disappeared from their line without a trace. I doubt it had anything to do with his stubbornness, do you?

I am planning a trip back to Connecticut this fall, for a Royce (and Rice) reunion and I am really looking forward to it. One of the high spots will be touring my 7th great grandfather's house, built in 1672 and still standing in Wallingford! Not too many folks can do that, I believe. I have been hearing a lot more whispering lately, (even as my hearing is deteriorating, badly), and I will be listening very intently in that old house!

How History Repeats Itself

by Eddie Lynn (Glitz) Davi
Red Oak, Texas

I find it curious that some children born today in our family have the names of our ancestors. Some have been ancestors we did not know existed until I started doing family research!

For example, my daughter named one of her children Rebecca

and we have since come to find out that my husband's Davis line has a grandmother Rebecca back in 1876.

One night when I was about 15 years old I had an amazing experience. My parents were asleep in their bedroom, which was quite far from my bedroom. I was dead asleep and woke up to an ice chill in the air. I opened my eyes and way across the room stood my uncle who had died about a year before. I shook my head and wouldn't believe what I was seeing because I did not have my glasses on. Before I knew it, he was gone again.

When I told my mom what I had seen she warned me to never tell anyone else, for they would think I had lost my mind. Not long before she died she admitted to me that she had also seen this uncle after he died.

My dad's mother died a year before I was born, so I never knew her. As a child I loved dolls and writing more than anything. One day while I was talking with my dad he told me that his mother had loved dolls so much that Grandpa was going to buy one of those fancy dolls to put on her gravesite. Dad talked him out of it because he thought someone would steal it. Then Dad talked about how much Grandmother liked to write stories.

Dad did not know I liked to do those things also. As I grow older I look more and more like this grandmother. Her name was Addie Opheila and guess what my real name is? Eddie Lynn—I was the last of the four girls born to my parents and they gave me dad's name. Just in the last 10 years did I associate my name Eddie being so close to Addie.

CHAPTER ASSIGNMENT:

Choose one of the web-sites mentioned in this chapter and explore for awhile. If you haven't already done so, complete your personal family group chart with yourself as both a child and a parent, if applicable. This will be your "nuclear family." Then create one for your siblings as parents, which will display your nephews and nieces.

_____

_____

_____

_____

_____

_____

_____

_____

_____

_____

_____

_____

CHAPTER 5

Turn Over A New Leaf

Dead ends and brick walls

As you spend more time researching your family history, there will be days when you feel like you have hit a brick wall and can't seem to go any farther in your research. You are sure to discover "Murphy's Laws" of genealogy.

If you haven't yet, here are a few of the delightful laws you can look forward to:

Murphy's Laws of Genealogy

Author Unknown

- The one and only document containing evidence of the missing link in your research will, invariably, be lost due to fire, flood, or war.
- Your great, great grandfather's obituary states that he died, leaving no issue of record.
- The critical link in your family tree is named "Smith."

- The town clerk you wrote to in desperation, and finally convinced to give you the information you need, can't write legibly, and doesn't have a copying machine.
- The Last Will and Testament you need is in the safe on board the "Titanic."
- That ancient photograph of four relatives, one of whom is your progenitor, carries only the names of the other three.
- Copies of old newspapers containing articles about your family have holes which only occur on last names.
- You learned that great aunt Beverly's Executor just sold her life's collection of family genealogical materials to a flea market dealer "somewhere in New York City."
- Yours is the ONLY last name not found among the three billion in the world-famous Mormon Church's archives in Salt Lake City, Utah.
- Ink fades and paper deteriorates at a rate inversely proportional to the value of the data recorded.
- After years of research and financial sacrifice you solve the family mystery only to hear your aunt say "I could have told you that!"

Some might say the catch phrase for this chapter is "I think that I shall never see a completed genealogy!" We'd rather say it is "When in doubt, keep moving!" There WILL be times when you hit that proverbial brick wall and can't seem to find the information you want. Don't give up. Maybe you just need to set that name aside and work on someone else for awhile. If it is true that the heavens are very interested in our earthly attempts at uniting families, then you must remember that it is a loving Heavenly Father whose timing has purpose. Listen to His promptings to guide you in your research. What you think is a brick wall may really be someone leading you somewhere else for a more important reason.

Compiled Records

Maybe you have already picked the pieces of genealogical "fruit" from the family tree that were easiest to reach, but you're still hungry for more. You want something you can really sink your teeth into, like biographical information or extended family names. Your next resource is to use compiled records, which means data collected by someone else who is willing to share it. You can find compiled genealogical records that are either published formally or just online. You can even find full pedigrees that seem to expand your own for several generations. Just when you think you've found a bulldozer for that brick wall, be careful to check the sources and documentations. Compiled records come from fallible genealogists, like us all.

Remember the key benefit in using compiled records is in sharing, not the perfection of the records. They may come in the form of narrative genealogies or lineage-linked formats.

Many websites have been created just to allow genealogists to share their information, reducing duplication while encouraging cooperation. The largest web site for compiled genealogies is www.familysearch.org. This is the official research site for the Church of Jesus Christ of Latter-day Saints. In this free website, patrons can search by surname or exact name to see what research has been done on an individual. All data has been submitted by patrons rather than professional genealogists, so there is no guarantee of accuracy. One small typo can change data substantially! However, contact information about the submitter of each record is available so that you can contact the researchers and ask questions about her resources.

Be sure to check out the USGenWeb Lineage Researcher pages at http://www.rootsweb.com/~lineage/ It is a wonderful web site where researchers who are looking for descendents of one particular ancestor can list their information. Links will include the ancestor's name, location, dates, a family web page (if there is one), and an e-mail address, so you can contact that person. It's a great place to find long lost living relatives, as well as connect with others who are either looking for the same information you are or who have already found it!

Search Engines

Another method for trying to break down the brick wall that blocks your research progress is using search engines. They allow you to just type in your ancestor's name and search for any sites which contain that name. They have huge indexes of information and can search the entire Internet for web pages related to your search request. An example of a genealogical search engine is www.genealogyportal.com. General information search engines include:

www.google.com
www.altavista.com
www.excite.com
www.ask.com
www.vivisimo.com

www.ixquick.com

www.dogpile.com

www.metacrawler.com

www.search.com

Other database search engines can be accessed only with a subscription fee such as www.ancestry.com or www.genealogy.com They charge monthly fees, but contain over 2 billion names and continue to update daily. More websites that contain genealogical indices, without charging fees for basic searches, include www.cyndislist.com, www. genealogyhomepage.com, and www.genealogytoolbox.com.

Surname Lists

It would be handy to write letters to anybody with your shared surname, but that would require a lot of money in postage and time researching phone books. Again, the wonderful technology of the Internet has become a genealogist's dear friend. It's like a master gardener climbing with you, as you try to learn more about your family tree. A quick and much less expensive way of communicating with a vast amount of people is in posting query letters on the Internet. Forums established just for and by genealogists exist to help people connect and share their research. An example is www.genforum.com. A comprehensive list of mailing lists is found on www.rootsweb.com. You can join mailing lists for your chosen surnames and receive correspondence related just to your names. So instead of climbing all of the trees in an orchard to see which ones are yours, you can use the Internet to tell you which trees are worth climbing and related to your family.

Professional Tree Climbers

They say the cheapest way to have your family tree traced is to run for public office! Now if you're truly getting tired of climbing trees or hitting your head against a brick wall, you may consider hiring a professional researcher for a fee.

To amateur genealogists, that would be like hiring someone to climb your family tree to tell you about the spectacular view from the top, which would spoil the adventure in it all! For those who still yearn to know about their family tree but truly don't have the time or patience, it is by no means "cheating" to use a professional. The area you are researching may just be too far for you to travel to or in a foreign language you are unfamiliar with.

Before hiring a professional genealogist, be sure to get references or a list of past customers. Check out the following for professional research services:

www.on.net/proformat/

www.familytree.hu

www.lineages.com/store/searches.asp

www.xmission.com/~tconcept/genhome.htm.

The stories in this chapter, as well as throughout this book, are meant to give you encouragement. They are true tales of patience, frustration, persistence and hope. Reading their stories can also be helpful, as you see how they tackled their research problems to arrive at their final destination. You just might pick up a tip that leads you in the right direction. Your story will have a happy ending too! Someone once said, "Only a genealogist regards a step backward as progress!"

The Brick Wall

by Cidney Engberg
Wheaton, Ilinois

We all encounter the "brick wall" in family research. I have never talked to any genealogist who has worked for years that hasn't hit one! I have a few times, but one experience stands out.

While searching for where my husband's grandmother was born in Finland, we took a road trip to the county in Michigan where her brother was living. We drove to the little town of Alpha and, grasping for straws, I went into the little post office and asked if there was anyone in town that was named Erickson or Jutila. The woman at the post office was so helpful and phoned an elderly man who had lived there all of his life and was considered to be the town historian. He said he vaguely remembered William Erickson and that he went to school with Andrew Jutila, husband of William's daughter, Sofia. He and Andrew were good friends.

He gave me a phone number to a lady who he thought might remember more about this family. When I called her she remembered a lot of things, but couldn't answer my burning question—where in Finland did the Erickson fellow come from? She talked about Andrew's brother-in-law who visited occasionally from the west coast. She mentioned that he had to come and settle the estate when Andrew died in 1985. She gave me his name and thought he could still be alive.

We drove back to the courthouse, where I had been looking earlier, and asked if there was a will or probate record for Andrew Jutila. Sure enough, there it was! I got a copy of it, which revealed the name and address of the brother-in-law! Using the Internet I found the phone number of that corresponding address in Washington state

*and picked up the phone. When I called I talked to a lovely man.
He said he had suffered a few strokes and his memory wasn't like it
should be, but he remembered visiting his in-law and remembered
William Erickson, who had passed away. He thought that the
Jutila family came from the Vassa area. I was elated! With just
that little bit of information I was later able to find many members
of the Jutila family.*

*I revel in finding such nice people to talk to, going to those little
towns where they lived, walking where they walked, and digging
through old records at the courthouse. My husband thinks it's a little
nuts when I say I feel more connected, but I do. Such wonderful
history and such good people, past and present.*

Trina had a similar experience during a genealogical search in
Salt Lake City:

God Bless Those Who Get In Your Way

*Every summer I try to visit Salt Lake City to see relatives and
squeeze in a trip to the world's largest genealogy library, owned
by the Church of Jesus Christ of Latter-day Saints. The library is
enormous and I always feel overwhelmed and a little lost while I
attempt to find information about my ancestors. Hours seem like
minutes inside the building and before I know it I've run out of
time. I had been working on a particular line on my husband's
side of the family one day, but without any luck. As I glanced at
the clock I realized I only had 30 minutes left to work before I'd
have to leave and pick up my children from the babysitter's house.
Because I only get to this wonderful library once a year I began to*

feel particularly frustrated, knowing that the information I needed had to be somewhere in that library! But where? I hit a brick wall.

I decided to switch the family line I was working on and began to look for a woman who was born in Boon County, Arkansas in 1860. The SLC library is so huge that I'm always impressed with myself whenever I can just find the correct part of the building that might carry the specific data I need. I finally found an aisle of books on Arkansas with census records. Unfortunately, they didn't have the 1860 census book I was hoping would be there, so I began my search on another shelf, mumbling a quick prayer to God that He might help me find what I needed. My plea was more of a grumpy whine than a prayerful petition. After all, HE knew where the information was, so why wouldn't He just help me out?

Suddenly a very large woman walked into the aisle where I was and sat herself right smack down in front of where I was looking. I was getting more anxious by the minute as the clock on the wall ticked my impending deadline. Now my search would be slowed down since I'd have to share these books with her. I managed to start some chit-chat with her and quickly learned she had been to Boon County only three months ago! She asked what I was looking for and, hearing of my unsuccessful search, she suggested that I try looking in the Carroll County census books. She explained that Boon County had once been a part of Carroll County many years ago. Well, how on earth would I have ever known that?

I thought it was certainly worth a try, so I knelt down and picked up the first book on the bottom shelf where those books happened to be. I'm sure my Heavenly Father chuckled, seeing me put in my place…on my knees. Very appropriate for such a cranky daughter who was about to receive an answer to prayer. I flipped through the pages of the book and my eyes popped wide open as I quickly found the ancestor I had been looking for! Not only was she listed on the page, but so was information about her parents and two other sisters who I didn't even know existed!

I hugged the woman, thanking her, convinced that a kind Heavenly Father had sent her to my aisle to get in my way and speed up my research!

A Breath of Fresh Air Can Do Wonders

by Ron Bremer
Paradise, Utah

When I was employed by the Genealogical Society of Utah, I was asked to locate the old records for the city of New York. There were a lot of current records, but not many of the really old records I was looking for. A lady in Long Island had told me about an old building that housed these elusive records in the basement. After looking half of the day through a basement full of records, without success, I decided to walk around the old building where I had been for a breath of fresh air and to clear my head.

Around the building was another entrance with a doorbell on the wall. To humor my curiosity, I pushed it and one of the panels in the wall opened up, which allowed me to walk down some rusty old stairs. I was now in a sub-basement, which had been built in the mid 1800s. Now I understood why I hadn't found anything in the basement! The really old records were in the sub-basement!

Two boiler men met me with large flash lights. I was the first visitor in years. They told me to follow them to the old records. It was dusty, dirty and dripping water everywhere. There were old rusty cans of war rations and lots of rats. After what seemed like a very long way, we came to a large room which had lots of large steel beams. Here were the old records in question. Some of them went clear back to the Dutch period of immigration to New York. We estimated that there were at least fifty tons of records in the great storage area. It was a miracle those records had survived through the years and that I actually could find them. Relentless sleuthing and a restless walk around the old building paid off.

Looking for Lies

by LeAnne Deardeuff
Jamesport, Missouri

After my grandmother died in 1966, my father, an avid genealogist, wanted to have a copy of her birth certificate. He searched fruitlessly for eight years. She had told him that she was born in 1900 in Middleboro, Warren County Ohio, but we could never turn up any documents on her or her family. My father would question his aunts and they would insist that Middleboro was her birthplace. We knew the names of Grandmother's brothers, sisters and parents from a family Bible that she had given to him; however, it did not contain their birthdates or their birthplaces.

Finally, one night my father had a dream. Grandma came to him and told him that she had lied. She said that she was actually older then Grandpa and that her name wasn't Lela, but was Rosa! My father jumped out of bed and had a sudden inspiration that she probably also lied about her birthplace. He grabbed a map of Ohio and realized that Middleboro was on the county line. Just a few miles away was the town of Clarksville in Clinton County, Ohio.

The next morning he called in to work and said that he wasn't going to be there that day. He asked my sister and me to skip school. We all went to the Family History Library in Salt Lake City, Utah for the day to search through microfilm. He handed me one to research that had birth certificates from Clarksville a few years earlier than Grandma said she was born. I tediously looked at birth certificate after birth certificate. It seemed as if there was a presence of someone standing over my left shoulder watching the film also.

Suddenly, a voice spoke to me. "Slow down," he said, "You have almost found me." Excitement welled up in my heart. All of a sudden, the name of a young boy came up on the screen. His parents were my great grandparents! He had died in infancy and was not recorded in the family Bible. He was my grandmother's oldest brother. His spirit shouted, "You found me!" I screamed out loud, "Dad come quick!" My father was sitting several desks away looking at another film and ran over excitedly. We wrote down the name of the boy, but then I knew that I needed to keep going. In the same film, I found that the next year my great grandparents had had another infant son, who had also died in infancy. He wasn't recorded in the family Bible either. Then I found my grandmother. She was two years older than she said she was and her name was Rosa May. That day we found the birth certificates of all her brothers and sisters. It was an exciting day, to say the least!

As a prologue to the story, my father went back to talk to his aunts to find out why they had all lied about their ages and birthplace. It turned out that my grandmother was two years older than my grandfather and she didn't want him to know. She had never liked her name even as a child and had been called Lela as a nickname.

So, when she got married she made a pact with her sisters that they would all change the dates of their births in order that they would be younger and she could be younger then her husband. So that no one would find out, they said they were born in the neighboring town. Her sisters kept that secret for over 60 years! My name is LeAnne, after my Grandmother Lela and her sister Anne!

CHAPTER ASSIGNMENT:

Write down the name of the ancestor who seems to be providing the biggest brick wall in your research. Now, write down some resources you haven't tried yet. Choose one that you will try this week.

_____

_____

_____

_____

_____

_____

_____

_____

CHAPTER 6

Climbing Trees And Skinned Knees

Creative ways to get your family involved

"There are only two lasting bequests we can give our children. One is roots; the other, wings."
—ANONYMOUS

When most people think of genealogy they imagine a lonely old woman, sitting quietly at a computer or reading dusty old books in the basement of a dark library with only cobwebs and a ticking clock for company. Doing family history research can definitely be a solitary activity, but it doesn't have to be! In fact, it's a lot more fun and meaningful when you involve the entire family! You've already read some stories in the first few chapters that showed researchers who dragged parents, spouses, and children along on their journey. Turn your family into detectives by including them in some of your genealogy tasks. By involving the whole family in your efforts, they will gain a greater sense of pride and love for their heritage. Besides, we all know that children love to climb trees!

One word of caution, however—if your genealogy quest is a fairly new one, you may need to be careful about how enthusiastically you try to recruit your family's help. One of us, who shall remain anonymous, had just started doing family history, and had an unbridled zeal for the work that was embarrassing, and downright obnoxious at times. At our aunt's funeral she ran around the funeral home exclaiming, "Oh! This is so great!"

Of course, she was referring to the wonderful gathering of relatives whom she could interview and collect new data from in one single day, however, not everyone in the room shared her enthusiasm for the sad occasion!

The following are some fun ways you can involve your living loved ones in the exciting hunt we call genealogy:

- Create a time capsule. Have your family members choose objects that represent what is important or typical in their lives. Place the objects in a storage box or "strongbox" to open 25 years from now or on a future date that has special meaning to your family.
- Create a "Funny Journal" where your family records all of the funny things you and your crazy relatives say. You could make a special journal for each member of the family or just use one book to record the collection of comical moments of your nutty family.
- Get involved in the USGenWeb Tombstone Project as a family. You can record tombstone data in a cemetery near where you live and submit it online so that other genealogists far away can have access to that data. To learn more about how you can join this important and worthwhile project go to http://www.rootsweb.com/~cemetery/
- Have your family take a culinary and cultural journey through

countries where your ancestors have lived. Talk about Great Grandma Kroescher while you eat bratworst and listen to German music. Serve teriyaki and wear paper shoes while you discuss Grandpa Larry who served in the military in Japan.

+ Find your ancestor's Coat of Arms or family crest. If you can't find it or don't have one then create your own, using free software at www. yourchildlearns.com/heraldry.htm Display it in your home or have it printed on shirts for the whole family to wear at your next reunion or family gathering!

+ Have the computer geek in your family set up a Yahoo News Group where relatives can post family news, create fun polls, upload photos, and share other items of interest related to a common ancestor.

+ Create a "Traditions" book for your family where you write down all of the traditions you share during the year. Be sure to record even the small things such as saying grace before dinner or when you always raise your soda pop bottles to make a toast for world peace. Have any special songs, stories or games been passed down in your family?

+ As your children grow older, ask them to choose one toy, book, clothing item or other special item that they would like to save for their future children.

+ Keep a video history of your family. Identify on the video the names of those pictured and the occasion for the recording.

+ Now is a great time to turn those old family movies on VHS into DVDs. They'll be easier to watch and store but, more importantly, protected against videotape that corrodes over the years. You can purchase equipment that uses your computer to transfer old tapes onto DVDs. It's expensive, but worth the investment considering that your family movies are priceless. Have a big movie night or start a new tradition of watching family movies every Sunday night while eating popcorn.

- Attend a genealogical event together as a family. There are all kinds of fun conferences, seminars and fairs all over the country. To find out about one in your area or even in a location you've always wanted a good excuse to visit go to http://www.genealogyshoppe.com/events.html

- For some cheap entertainment, check out www.alsirat.com/epitaphs where you can read amusing epitaphs such as "I told you I was sick", found on a tombstone in a Utah cemetery.

- Gather favorite family recipes and create a special family recipe book. Invite extended relatives to share their favorite dishes and even write down stories about the best cooks in the family and memorable meals shared together. These special recipe books make great wedding presents and Christmas gifts.

- Have your children create some kind of keepsake to give to everyone at your next family reunion.

- Design family placemats by creating a collage of photos, drawings, news articles or other information about each person. Be sure to laminate the placemat before putting any food on it! These might make great gifts as well as fun decorations for your next family event.

- If you trace back far enough, you're sure to find a famous ancestor. Read books and biographies about that person. If you're lucky, there may even be a movie about him or her!

- You say your great grandpappy died of Anasarca and Great Aunt Darla had a terrible case of Kruchhusten? To learn about old medical terms, check out this web page: http://www.rootsweb.com/~usgwkidz/oldmedterm.htm
- Create a web site for your family where relatives can upload photos, news, and other things that interest the group. Provide links to web sites that extended family members have also created.
- Watch a movie about the country where one of your ancestors came from.
- If you qualify, join the Sons or Daughters of the American Revolution. Another cool organization is the Sons of the Union Veterens of the Civil War. Did you know they both have special presentations their members will make for free at a Court of Honor when your son earns the Eagle Scout Award? Very impressive.
- Plan a family reunion! There are tons of great ideas on the Internet, as well as books, that give you creative ideas for games, invitations, ice-breakers, food, and other activities that can become the newest tradition for you and your relatives. Read chapter 10 for more ideas and "how to's."
- Design family T-shirts that everyone could wear in a family photo or at a family reunion.
- Begin a family newsletter that could be sent to all of your relatives. Include family updates and photos. You could create a "Round Robin" newsletter which is started by one family and then passed on to another who then adds their news and then passes it along to another and so on, until it makes its way back to the originating family, who starts another one!

+ Have your family learn about the USGen Web Project at www. usgenweb.org. Click on to the link for the state where you live or where you're searching for an ancestor. Find out how you can volunteer or get involved with one of their wonderful projects.

+ Have your family write a skit or practice a special musical number they can perform at your next family reunion. Write a play about one of your ancestors or even about a descendent who hasn't been born yet and how he might live and view your crazy traditions!

+ Learn the mother tongue of your ancestors. Practice using your new language together as a family.

+ Hang photographs of ancestors on the wall, rather than keeping them boxed up or put away in a scrapbook. Create a family wall somewhere in the house or down a hallway.

+ Have someone paint a tree as a mural on a wall somewhere in your home. On the leaves write names of your relatives or hang small family photos on the branches.

+ Create a visual family tree by hanging photographs in the style of a pedigree chart.

+ Have your family create a written inventory of the videos and DVDs you already have of your family.

+ Create a timeline for your family or of a particular ancestor's life.

+ Learn how to do tombstone rubbings at
http://www.angelfire.com/ky2/cemetery/art.html
To learn about the meanings of tombstone carvings go to
http://www.palmettoroots.org/Tombstones.html

+ Join mailing lists for people who are doing genealogy like you. There are lists just for youngsters, moms, teenagers, etc. who want to compare notes and share their challenges and triumphs.

* Instead of spending money on toys and gadgets that will end up on a shelf or on the garage sale table, get your family in the habit of giving genealogy-minded gifts.

* Find out what holiday traditions there are for the country of your family's origin and begin incorporating some of those customs into how your family celebrates each year.

* Have your children check out http://www.aecf.org/kidscount/ census/ where they can learn about census data online and create their own reports!

* Watch the landmark TV miniseries *Roots* together as a family. Let Alex Haley's quest for heritage inspire you to discover yours.

* Go to http://www.last-names.net/Articles/Anatomy.asp to learn about the meaning of your name and read about the anatomy of a surname. This web site also shows which names are the most popular in this country and around the world.

* Ever wonder what epidemics your ancestors survived or exactly how widespread the disease was that did take their lives? See an interesting chart of America's health at http://www.rootsweb. com/~usgwkidz/epidemic.htm Talk with your family about your medical heritage.

* If you live near a naval base or seaport you can often find companies that provide tours and excursions on old ships, similar to one your ancestor may have traveled on. Imagine what your ancestor might have experienced in cramped quarters or feel that salt air on your face. Sometimes they have special trips you can sign up for where you get to spend the night or be a "crewmember" for a day.

- As your family looks at census reports you may run across strange occupations such as Keeler or Birlyman. To learn what those are, and many more, click on to http://www.rootsweb.com/~usgwkidz/ oldjobs.htm   Does your family have a certain line of work that has been passed down from one generation to another?

- Learn how to do a craft that your ancestors did, such as tatting, crocheting, knitting, whittling, etc.

- Have family members keep a personal journal. Remember, a birth certificate proves that you were born. A death certificate proves that you died. But a personal history proves and shows that you lived!

- Plant an old English herb garden in honor of your British ancestors.

- When your children have to write a report for school, help them add a personal element to the research by sharing information about a particular ancestor and the political or economical environment during a particular time period.

- For the fashion-minded teenage girls in your family, learn about the styles that your ancestors might have worn. Have an old-fashioned fashion show!

- Take your children to visit a cemetery where an ancestor was buried and leave flowers or other meaningful items at the gravesite. Rather than focusing on the death, talk about the great contributions that person made to your family's heritage.

- Write a letter to an ancestor, describing what a typical day is like in your life. Compare it to what might have occurred in that person's life. A writing exercise like this could be preserved in a special genealogy journal and will be priceless to generations yet unborn.

- Take a family trip to Ellis Island in New York to look at the authentic immigration passenger lists. Be sure to visit the Statue of Liberty and imagine how your ancestor might have felt stepping onto the shores of America for the first time.

- For a somber, yet meaningful family experience, talk about what you would like written on your epitaph when you die. Discuss how you would like your funeral to be. Make sure family wishes are known regarding memorial services, gravesite care, casket viewing, and will execution. Ok, so this idea doesn't exactly qualify to be on a list of "fun family activities", but sooner or later you're going to need to talk about this stuff!

- Plan a family vacation to historical spots in America, including battlegrounds, presidential libraries, homes of famous patriots, and national monuments.

- Create a genetic pedigree chart and see if you can determine which family members passed along the physical traits that make your family unique. Which relatives had similar noses or smiles? Which characteristic is repeated most often? Which characteristic will future children most likely inherit?

- Film a video of your family introducing themselves to future generations. Show a tour of your home. Sing a song or tell jokes! Have family members interview each other or just let the camera keep running while you all sit together and talk about your life.

- Make a quilt using handprints of family members in each square. Dip hands in paint or trace fabric around your loved ones' hands to get the size. Be sure to identify who the hands belong to and the date.

+ Save the newspaper from the day each family member was born. If you don't have them you can write to the newspaper in that city and get a copy from their archives.

+ Watch an episode of the wonderful PBS series _Ancestors_ together.

+ Attend religious services at the church or synagogue where your ancestors attended. Learn about their religion and talk about your family's spiritual heritage.

+ Buy a fire safety box and spend some time gathering important documents that could be kept there. Fire boxes are also great places to store photo negatives, old coins, passports, heirloom pieces, and other priceless momentos.

+ This year do something really special for Grandparents Day. Yes, it's a fairly new holiday, but it's a good one! Honor your grandparents and let them know you truly appreciate the legacy they have given you.

+ Encourage children to start a "Cousins Club" where all of the cousins can plan activities and future trips together, e-mail one another, and get to know each other better.

+ Make puppets that resemble family members and create a puppet show that your family could perform at your next big family gathering. See if the audience can guess who the puppets are.

+ Host a contest for extended family on your family website or at a reunion, where relatives can write an essay on a particular genealogy topic or aspect of your family heritage. Judges select the winning entries, awarding prizes and certificates to all who participate.

+ Add the dates of your favorite ancestors' birthdays to your calendar and bake a cake in their honor. Hey, any excuse to eat cake, right?

+ Encourage family members to begin writing their autobiography. Give them an assignment each week to write about a certain aspect of their life, such as dating years, school days, employment history, etc.

+ Have older children and family members help identify items from an estate inventory, recording names, dates, and other important information.

+ In our family, Brittany is our creative filmmaker, who carries the camcorder around during vacations with extended family. She films the activities and all the crazy things the relatives do during the trip. Later, she edits the film, adding music and silly captions, creating an entertaining movie that even Steven Spielberg would be proud of. We always look forward to the unveiling of her masterpiece the next time we get together. If you don't have a teenager in your family who is responsible with the equipment then assign yourself the task of family filmmaker! There is such a great selection of movie-making software nowadays, that anyone can learn how to do it!

+ Create a talking journal by recording relatives on audio-cassette.

+ Create "Memory Triggers" by writing down places, scenarios, song titles, and other things on slips of paper. Play a game where family members take turns pulling the "memory triggers" out of a box and then telling a story from their life about the words on the paper.

+ Find out what famous people were born on the same day as your family members. You can also find out what historical events occurred that day by going to www.scopesys.com/today/

+ Using a large map, identify all of the cities and states where current and/or past family members have resided or traveled.

- Visit a Family History Center together, located in the Church of Jesus Christ of Latter-day Saints.
- Play a home-made version of the game show "Jeopardy," with categories about your family history such as: "The Way We Were", "Kids Will Be Kids", "Wedding Bells", "School Days", etc.
- Have everyone write in their journals for 10 minutes every night before bedtime.
- Make a Bible pedigree chart, showing the genealogies of Adam, Noah, Jesus, or any other person in the scriptures that your family would like to study.
- Create a family phone tree for emergencies.

If all of those ideas aren't enough to get your creative juices flowing, then check out the following web sites for more fun genealogy activities that will inspire kids:

http://www.rootsweb.com/~usgwkidz/

www.worldalmanacforkids.com

http://scout.wisc.edu/Projects/PastProjects/

http://genealogy.allinfoabout.com/subjects/subgen_kids.html

http://www.genealogytoday.com/junior/

Spiritual Spell-Check

by Denise Parsons
McHenry, Illinois

I find it so interesting that others have felt the spiritual and calm feelings that so often have kept me at my computer, researching families for hours on end. I have been researching genealogy and family stories for 35 years now and have volumes of information. One of the more important aspects of my project is when I feel the presence of individuals who seem to guide me to the right spelling of a surname or the right town, which enables me to match up families.

I am a Hospice Nurse and at the end of a tough day, I look forward to fussing at my genealogy in hopes that I can draw on the warmth that seems to surround me when I am looking for someone special.

CHAPTER ASSIGNMENT:

Think of a family member who you would like to involve in your family history research. What are his special interests hobbies? How could you recruit his help, using his talents and interests?

_____

_____

_____

_____

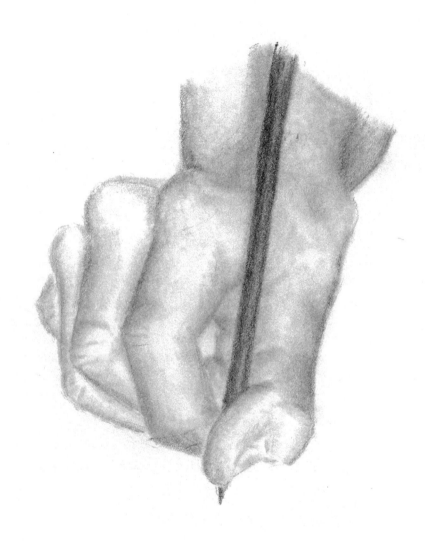

CHAPTER 7

Going Out On A Limb
And Avoiding False Footings
Documentation and joining genealogical societies

Realtors have an axiom—location, location, location. The genealogical corollary to that is—documentation, documentation, documentation! Just because you read something on the Internet or have copied something down from a newspaper to put in your files, doesn't mean it's fact! Genealogists often say "Without proof there is no truth!" Of course, that comment can't be verified, so don't take our word for it.

Be sure to document your sources for everything and know the difference between primary sources (original documents and living witnesses to events) and secondary sources (printed books or a distant cousin's hearsay). Without proof, your genealogy research becomes mythology. The wise genealogist will always check documents for accuracy, especially when sharing information online. All it takes is one careless typo to send you off in the wrong direction! When you keep notes in your research log, be sure to mention which data is fact and which is speculation; that will help to prevent you from going down the wrong path in the future. When in doubt, cite your source. When there is no doubt, cite your source!

You might wonder what all of the fuss is about and why you have to go through the hassle of documenting everything. If you're like most people, the time you spend doing your genealogy is found in small snippets, in between everything else you do in your life. You think you'll never forget that book where you found Uncle Bradley's real estate records, but in a few years when you need that information again you might not be able to recreate it. You don't want to have to reinvent the wheel every time you want to find that particular data on Great Grandpa Larry's car (mediocre pun intended.)

Genealogical societies exist to make your family history research easier. They do this by working hard at preserving records, as well as by making them available to as many people as possible. All records are threatened by the natural aging process, and many need to be indexed, transcribed or microfilmed. Those things cost money! Besides helping genealogical research in general, a paid membership into a society can also help you contact others who share your research, meet other family historians and hear informative speakers who can help your research.

Whether you are a just a weekend genealogist or a professional who gets paid to research other people's family history, there is always something new to learn. Get out of your research rut by taking a genealogy class, attending a conference, reading a new genealogy book or learning about a new research skill online.

Subscribe to Listservs on the Internet for your localities and interests to meet people with the same background. Sign up on common genealogy website query pages at rootsweb.com, ancestry.com, USGenweb, etc.

Expanding your research techniques by using such resources really helps you to "go out on a limb" farther than if you just stick to one way of doing your genealogy.

Automatically downloading or copying information from various resources without verifying their documentation can lead to false footings. A risky practice by many, who are anxious to extend their own pedigree chart, is to simply copy an existing pedigree from a computer source and download it into your database as fact. That other chart may contain many errors. Until you can get documentation on newly shared information, don't merge it with your own material. In this day and age of computer worms and virus, you'll also want to make sure the files are clean and safe before adding them to your work. Better safe than sorry!

Using family relations to collect stories and data is an extremely helpful resource, but be careful not to rely on family folklore as fact. Note it as such in your own documentation as "family legend says…", or "a story told by Uncle Tom is…" Names, dates, and even pronunciations can change important details as an oral history evolves. For years, we spoke of Uncle Harm, only to learn later that his name was really Hiram—our relatives' southern accent altered our understanding of his correct name!

After being appropriately cautious in your note taking, don't disregard all hearsay either. Those traditional tales from relatives are what make the biographies so colorful and fun! They say that genealogists never die; they just lose their census . . .

The Census Taker

By Darlene Caryl-Stevens
Spokane, Washington

It was the first day of census, and all through the land,
The pollster was ready, a black book in hand.
He mounted his horse for a long dusty ride;
His book and some quills were tucked close by his side.
A long winding ride down a road barely there,
Toward the smell of fresh bread wafting up through the air.
The woman was tired with lines on her face,
And wisps of brown hair she tucked back into place.
She gave him some water, as they sat at the table;
And she answered his questions—the best she was able.
He asked of her children. Yes, she had quite a few;
The oldest was twenty, the youngest not two.
She held up a toddler with cheeks round and red;
His sister, she whispered, was napping in bed.
She noted each person who lived there with pride;
And she felt the faint stirrings of the wee one inside.
He noted the sex, the color, the age.
The marks from the quill soon filled up the page.
At the number of children, she nodded her head;
And saw her lips quiver for the three that were dead.
The places of birth she "never forgot";

Was it Kansas? or Utah? or Oregon—or not?
They came from Scotland, of that she was clear;
But she wasn't quite sure just how long they'd been here.
They spoke of employment, of schooling and such;
They could read some, and write some, though really not much.
When the questions were answered, his job there was done;
So he mounted his horse and he rode toward the sun.
We can almost imagine his voice loud and clear;
"May God bless you all for another ten years."
Now picture a time warp—it's now you and me;
As we search for the people on our family tree.
We squint at the census and scroll down so slow,
As we search for that entry from long, long ago.
Could they only imagine on that long ago day,
That the entries they made would affect us this way?
If they knew, would they wonder at the yearning we feel,
And the searching that makes them so increasingly real.
We can hear if we listen the words they impart,
Through their blood in our veins and their voice in our heart.

Sharing Lessons Learned

by Diane Bernota Rooney
San Francisco, California

Like life itself, family history is a journey that follows a long and winding road. I have been working on my Lithuanian family history for eleven years now, and would like to end by sharing ten especially useful research tips that have helped me.

Most of these tips you have heard before, but I recommend them again because they can be invaluable:

⋅ *Talk to your living relatives repeatedly about their lives and what they remember about deceased family members. The memories of older family members are like a well that never runs dry. Each time you ask, you'll hear something new that they thought wasn't worth mentioning. Always ask about documents and photographs—I learned this one the hard way!*

⋅ *Use online mailing lists and bulletin boards. They have been absolutely invaluable in providing history, context, helpful research techniques, look-ups, and have even coughed up cousins and former neighbors.*

⋅ *Travel to research locations in the United States and elsewhere if at all possible. No one will be as diligent and committed to finding a record as you.*

⋅ *Try all possible spellings of your family names and keep track of the ones you try. The Ellis Island database is probably the best thing to happen to family historians since the Latter-day Saints discovered microfilm; but be aware that there are spelling variants both in the transcriptions and in the passenger records vs. the spellings used by your ancestors in Lithuania or elsewhere.*

⋅ *Use a Web search engine, such as www.google.com, to search for family names, including collateral lines, and places associated with your family. Follow up on leads, however unlikely: I found a wonderful cousin who came up as an author of many scientific papers. I checked the e-mail format for his company, e-mailed him, and heard back within ten minutes.*

⋅ *Save names and facts about people who had or could have had any type of affiliation with your family members: neighbors, fellow parishioners, classmates, coworkers, fraternal or civic association members, even hobbyists.*

Follow up on witnesses to civil and religious documents, as very often they are connected in some way and likely to turn up again.

• *Copy photographs and documents with a digital camera. Many fragile documents cannot be put in a copy machine, and photocopies of photographs are generally of poor quality in clarity and detail. Most places will let you use a digital camera without flash as it does not harm the original. An additional advantage is the ability to enlarge and lighten or darken the photograph or document, a great help with identification and handwriting analysis.*

• *Develop a sense of the context of your ancestors' lives and how that context influenced them. Read about political and religious activities, wars, disease and epidemics, economic data such as crop failures, types of work available, cost of living, and degree of industrialization, educational opportunities available, literacy rates, and transportation patterns, to name a few contextual factors that influenced our ancestors' lives. This will give you insights into why they emigrated, why they settled where they did, as well as the communities they lived in.*

• *Remember that family history works on karmic principles. If you help people with searches and spend time guiding newcomers, you will be infinitely repaid.*

 CHAPTER ASSIGNMENT:

Join a genealogical society or an online surname group this week!

CHAPTER 8

In The Leafy Treetops

Honoring heritage with crafts, photos, and decor

There is a children's song about birds that sing in the leafy treetops. The birds are the decoration and music of the beautiful trees. While we work on our family tree and fill out the leaves with names of loved ones, the decoration in the treetops becomes what we do with all of that good information. Every family has its own song. The music is the rich melody of our unique heritage that makes us dance!

Please don't tell us you are spending hours upon hours of research just to fill out a pedigree chart to put in a binder or drawer! Making your family's history come alive is the fun part! Genealogy is a living, breathing work that is never finished. With every new marriage vow and each baby's birth it grows and changes. As long-lost cousins are discovered and old relationships restored, there is much to celebrate! There are so many creative things you can do and make to honor your heritage and celebrate your family's unique place in this world. This chapter will give you a few ideas to help get your own creative juices flowing. We would love to hear what your families are doing to sing!

- Create a Coat of Arms for your family to display or give as gifts to relatives. If your family doesn't have one then create your own, using free software at www.yourchildlearns.com/heraldry.htm. Display it in your home or have it printed on shirts for the whole family to wear at your next reunion or family gathering!

- Hold a contest at your next family reunion or on your family's web site, where relatives can submit essays about a common ancestor, your family's homeland, or another aspect about your family's heritage. Judges select winners and all participants receive some kind of award or certificate.

- Design printed family trees that display your pedigree in a beautiful way. You can make your own or even buy one from www.ancestry.com where you get to choose from a variety of frames, styles, sizes, backgrounds and fancy paper.

- Create Christmas ornaments by using mini frames with photos inside or by making special ornaments out of quilted pieces of special fabric used for weddings, baby blankets, or another special event.

- Decoupage boxes, benches, or even dressers by using copies of special photographs, drawings or other cutouts that have special meaning to the family's history.

- Build or create a special trunk where family history items can be stored.

- Design a calendar using family photos for each month. Include birthdates of important ancestors and other special family history events.

- Make quilts or pillows using photos that have been transferred to fabric. What a great wedding present! Use recent photos or, better yet, present a quilt to the new bride in the family, using a photo from her great grandparents' wedding!

+ Use copies of family photographs or drawings to design greeting cards.

+ On this year's Christmas cards use pictures of ancestors! With cool software programs, like Photoshop, you can cut and paste an old picture of Great Grandpa Alfred so that he's sitting right next to baby Benjamin!

+ Buy a shadow box at your favorite craft store and fill it with pictures and heirloom items of one of your ancestors to either display on a table or hang on a wall.

+ If you're going to buy a new table for your living room, consider buying one of those shadow-box tables! Fill it with genealogy-related items for all to enjoy every day!

+ Have your family create self-portraits to hang on the wall. For some real cheap entertainment, have them draw pictures of each other to hang!

+ Gather favorite family recipes and create a genealogy recipe book.

+ Make your own diaries by using copies of pictures of ancestors to design the front cover and illustrate other pages throughout the book.

+ Roll lipstick on everyone's lips and have them all leaving their kissing imprint on special paper that will be framed. The design border around everyone's kisses could be in the shape of a heart, family tree, or even house. Have fun guessing whose lips are whose or have the kissers sign their name next to their now famous lips.

- Using family photographs, have computer mouse-pads made for family members to use and remind them about doing their genealogy when they sit down at their desk.
- There are all kinds of companies out there that will turn your photographs into coffee mugs, plastic plates, key chains and other fun products.
- Buy some of that poster paper that comes on rolls and make a time-line of your family's history.
- What's in a name? Using calligraphy, create a framed picture with a family member's name and the historic meaning of that name.
- Create a time capsule on someone's birthday, including items that represent that person's talents, interests and activities. Write a letter and have the time capsule opened on a future birthday.
- Using a large map, identify all of the cities and states where current and/or past family members have resided or traveled.
- Put a light behind a person's head to shine on to black paper and draw their profile.
- Create a music CD of songs that are especially important and meaningful to your family.
- Take a picture of just the men in the family. Dress them up and make them feel really important. Make another photo with just the girls.
- Make a Bible pedigree chart, showing the genealogies of Adam, Noah, Jesus, or any other person in the scriptures that your family would like to study.

- Create a love storybook for your family, gathering all love letters past, present and future into one romantic collection.
- Choose a family mission statement that can be written in lovely handwriting to display in the home or cross-stitch the words onto a pillow or something that can be framed.
- Create a family party book where you write down all of the things your family does throughout the year to celebrate holidays, birthdays, anniversaries, baptisms, any other special occasions.
- Write down all of your family's unique traditions. How do you chop down your Christmas tree? What do you do with that yule log? Who cuts the turkey at Thanksgiving? Don't forget to write down daily traditions, such as who says grace at dinner or how many kisses on the cheek Mom gets at bedtime?
- Instead of throwing away all those old jeans the kids outgrow or wear out, cut out some large pieces from the fabric and turn them into decorative pillows or even a fun picnic blanket! You'll have a memory of their favorite clothes and a casual home décor item that is sure to be a conversation-starter.
- Hang photographs of ancestors on the wall, rather than keeping them boxed up or put away in a scrapbook. Create a family wall somewhere in the house or down a hallway.
- Have someone paint a tree as a mural on a wall somewhere in your home. On the leaves write names of your relatives or hang small family photos on the branches.
- Create a visual family tree by hanging photographs in the style of a pedigree chart.

Once you've made your climb through the branches to the treetops, it's rewarding to see the great vista from the top. You can survey the view for a better overall perspective of your family tree. Perhaps even some genetics make more sense after studying several generations. There is an awesome reverence for family as you begin to see hundreds of names that represent real people who have lived life's lessons and brought you to where you are now. You honor them by the very act of collecting those names into one whole.

If you haven't begun to write biographies yet, now is the time. You have been enriched by your heritage hunting and now is the time to share that wealth of knowledge for the next generation. There are many books and computer programs available to help you write your own autobiography and/or biographies of your family. Including photos throughout any life history deepens the visual image of who that ancestor was.

A quick word on photographs. A picture is worth a thousand documents. They are priceless and need our utmost care. The worst places to store your photographs are in un-insulated attics or basements, and yet that is where most of us keep them! Constantly changing temperatures and humidity levels throughout the year can cause your photos to become brittle and crack. In severe cases, it may cause separation of the emulsion (image) from the support (paper base) of the photo. Dampness can cause photos to stick together.

Insects and rodents can feed on the photos or leave their droppings on your precious memories. The best place for storing photos is in a location with a constant temperature from 65 degrees to 70 degrees with low humidity. Don't store your negatives in the same place as your photos. In order to have a second chance of recovering damaged pictures, the best place to keep negatives are in those fire-safety boxes; even if the entire house burns down, you'll be able to make copies of your photos again.

Don't write on the back of the photos with a standard ball-point or felt-tip pen, because the acids in the ink could eat away and leave stains on your photos. Either find an acid-free photo marking pen or write lightly with a soft lead pencil.

If Winston Churchill did genealogy he would have said "Never, never, never throw away photos!" Before tossing out old photos that you don't want, offer them to other relatives! You don't get permission to throw them away, even if you don't know who is in the pictures. Donate them to antique stores or better yet, post them on the Internet so others can find them! Doing genealogy is all about sharing! There are quite a few websites online where you can post photos of your strangers, as well as hunt for photos of your ancestors. Many of the web sites also offer heirloom items that have been lost from their families. Here are a few sites you can check out:

www.deadfred.com
www.ancestorarchive.com
www.yourfamilyfinds.com
http://uk.geocities.com/ancestralpast/
www.adoptaphoto.com
http://www.familyworkings.com/links/photo.htm
www.civilwarmysteries.com (Civil War photos)
http://brylling.homepage.nu/ (Swedish photos)
www.pastconnect.com

The life expectancy of older color photos is anywhere from 20 to 60 years, but newer color pictures can be expected to last 100 years, due to the use of better printing techniques. Black and white pictures can last over 100 years. Of course, the lifespan of photos today depends on the quality of both the paper and ink that are used. Recruit your family's computer nerd to scan pictures into your computer and put them on to a CD. Add a little bit of music and it becomes a great presentation to show at your next family reunion, not to mention terrific gifts! With technology today there are so many great things you can do to enhance old photographs and use them in new creations.

It doesn't matter how you choose to organize your photographs, whether it be by theme or chronological order, by family member, or some other method. The important thing is to protect them from elements that will damage them, such as the sun, acids, or even careless fingers. The MOST important thing is to enjoy them!

A Picture is Worth a Thousand Words

by Carolyn Paulson

One of my favorite experiences concerns an old photograph. I was searching for information about John Thomas Booher. He was my 2nd great grandfather from Pope County, Arkansas. I discovered that a family had submitted information for a John Thomas Booher as a grandfather, but no other information was given. I contacted the family and told them that I did not know anything about my John Thomas Booher, except that I had an old, faded photograph of him with my Grandpa Booher. The name John Thomas Booher was written on the back. They told me that they also had a photograph of their John Thomas Booher. Knowing how difficult it can be to compare old photos, I was not very hopeful that we would be able to prove the photographs were of the same person. I made an appointment and took my photo to their home. They were a wonderful family and we chatted for awhile. Finally, they brought out their photo. It was an exact copy of mine! My newly found cousin died two months later.

Tracey had the following experience while spending a day organizing her parents' books:

A Love Story Revealed

One afternoon I was organizing some bookshelves in the office of my parents' home. I would read each book title and judge its future existence in mere seconds. Was it worthy to stay on our family bookshelf or would we generously donate it to the Salvation Army? I developed a quick pattern of looking at the book title, dumping it in the give-away box and then picking up the next book for the next instant judgment. It seemed most of the books were easily qualified for the charity box and not our shelf.

Another small, dull-colored, torn, paperback book was in my hands facing its judgment day. The title was: "Private Letters of the World's Great Lovers". "Probably another trashy, useless paperback," I thought. "I'll donate it. Wait. Hmmm, I wonder who qualifies as a World's Great Lover?"

Before placing it in the overflowing box of useless literature, I randomly focused on the name John Churchill, who wrote two letters to his wife Sarah Jennings. My eyes dilated, my eyebrows lifted and my mind raced to identify why those names seemed so oddly familiar. Where had I recently read their names? Then with a rapid race to my Book of Remembrance and a frantic flip of some pages I found their names included on a recently compiled chart I had received only a few weeks earlier from a distant relative. The chart had become neglected due to my lack of time to properly scrutinize the names and dates. Good ole John Churchill and Sarah Jennings were my own kin and I almost threw them away to their literary death! The book instantly became valued above all books I was keeping on the shelf.

As I thought about the coincidence of finding these love letters in a little insignificant book, my heart burned as if to correct my thought. Because I was the only one working on my family's genealogy at the time, if anyone else had been performing this book-sorting task, they would not have been able to identify the names, assuming the book would have opened to the exact page as it had for me. It seemed John and Sarah themselves had almost jumped into my face as if to remind me that they were a part of me, as well as my family's history. They wanted to be remembered for more than just their vital statistics. Their love and their lives will never be forgotten.

Enough Information

by Sherry Ann Miller

Gathering family names for genealogy is the heartbeat of my life, and has been for the past twenty years. Searching for my husband's ancestors introduced me into the world of genealogy briefly in the 1970's. In 1985, I came upon a goldmine of information and, for the first time in my life, I began researching family names in true earnest.

Although I've learned that it is important to keep track of dates and places, the stories behind the names I've found have astounded me time and again. Yet, it isn't the number of names I've gathered or my ancestors' precious stories that I've found that have kept me searching these past two decades. It is the inspirational experiences that have set my soul on fire…

Ignoring my father's parental line for the most part, I assumed that my uncle or his diligent cousin would get their genealogy finished, while I concentrated first on my mother's ancestors. Apparently, my plan of action did not suit Dad's paternal grandmother, Mary Ann Jollow, who died before I turned four years old. To be truthful, I don't remember ever meeting Mary Ann Jollow, even if I did, but I remembered her voice!

One spring morning, I walked into my den, thinking about all the names I planned to research that day, when I heard a woman's voice as crisp and clear as if she were standing right there beside me. "Sherry Ann!" she said. "You have enough information in your den to find my family!" Immediately, I knew the voice I heard had come from my great grandmother, Mary Ann Jollow.

Startled, I gasped aloud in surprise. A tingling sensation of warmth and certainty spread over me, from the top of my head to the tip of my toes. Her expectation had come without warning, and I began to look around my den to see where the information could be located. I had dozens of books on Mama's ancestors and one Book of Remembrance on Dad's father's line, but I didn't have anything on Mary Ann Jollow's extended family. Not one book, not one note, not one scrap of paper.

Puzzled, and a bit bewildered, I wondered where in my den I was supposed to search. Opening my genealogical software program, I looked up Great Grandmother Mary Ann Jollow, and found that *her father, Richard Jollow, had moved his family from England to Wales, sometime before she married Charles Stone in 1879.*

As I sat staring at my computer screen, wondering what could possibly be in my den that would help me find the Jollow family, my mind was enlightened and Great Grandma's words were verified. I was looking straight at it! My computer!

Immediately, I went online to www.Rootsweb.com and joined the Glamorgan, Wales E-mail list. As soon as I'd registered, I sent the list this query:

> I am searching for any Jollow descendants whose ancestors may have lived in Glamorgan, Wales, in the middle to late 1800's. My second great grandfather, Richard Jollow, lived in Llantrisant sometime between 1865 and 1900 when he died there.
>
> Any assistance you can share would be greatly appreciated.
>
> Best regards, Sherry Ann Miller

I sent the query off, thinking perhaps in a few days, or weeks, or even months, someone might respond. To my utter astonishment, an answer came back almost immediately, while I was still online looking for other ways of finding my Jollow ancestors. A woman sent me an e-mail to report that she lived in Llantrisant, around the corner from some Jollows, and if I would give her more information, she would be happy to contact them and see if we were related. Gladly, I gave her my name, phone number, and all the information I had on Richard Jollow's daughter, Mary Ann, and her husband, Charles Stone. Then, turning the computer off, I went into the kitchen to start lunch for my husband.

When the telephone rang, I answered it quickly, and felt a sweet and tingling sensation sweep through me once again. A woman with a heavy Welsh accent said, "Is this Sherry Ann Miller?" "Yes, it is." "My name is Dianne Jollow. I live in Llantrisant, Glamorgan, Wales, with my husband, Ray Jollow. You've been trying to find some Jollows in Llantrisant?"

"I am!" I exclaimed. "Are you related to Mary Ann Jollow?" To my relief and delight, she said, "Mary Ann was my husband's grand aunt. Ray came through her brother, William Jollow. In fact, we live in the house that William's father, Richard Jollow, built in the nineteenth century."

Her husband's family had always wondered what became of Mary Ann Jollow. Some said she married and went to America. Others said she died young and had no family, but no one could find a death record. They had been searching for Mary Ann for quite some time. Years earlier, they had gathered all the other Jollow information they could find, hoping to present their descendants with their compilation of The Jollow History. Their neighbor, who gave them my telephone number, was an answer to their prayers.

As they pieced the final puzzle together into their family genealogy, they shared their earlier labors and documentation with me. A simple message from beyond the veil, delivered to me by my great grandmother, Mary Ann Jollow, was true. I found enough information in my den to find her Jollows . . .and rather quickly!

CHAPTER ASSIGNMENT:

Choose a creative way to display old family photos in your home this week. If your genealogy software allows photos, insert what photos you have in the corresponding ancestors' file folders.

CHAPTER 9

Planting Trees

Sharing genealogical data with others

While you climb your family tree you can also be dropping fruitful seeds along the way. Your paper trail of research notes may become the well-marked path for another researcher in the future. Someone once said, "Take nothing but ancestors. Leave nothing but records."

In addition to the many positive qualities that genealogists are known for, such as persistence, faithfulness, and dogged tenacity, is their impressive spirit of sharing. It is the foundation of many genealogical societies. One of the most effective and well-known Internet sites for genealogists to connect with others who are researching the same surname is www.rootsweb.com.

By subscribing to a surname list you begin conversations that may lead you to family connections. Research groups are also made up of people researching similar surnames or looking in specific geographical locations. The most well known sites are:

GeneaSearch Surname Registry located at www.geneasearch.com/

surnameregister.htm and SurnameWeb at www.surnameweb.com.

Geographical societies include the Federation of Genealogical Societies at www.familyhistory.com/societyhall/

Federation of Family History Societies at www.ffhs.org.uk.

Joining formal family associations may also lead you to a group with formal organization of research efforts and even finding some long-lost cousins. What you consider basic information on your immediate or extended family could be the long-lost treasure to someone else. Sharing information benefits all of us. Be cautious about sharing personal information about people who are still alive in order to protect both their privacy and security.

Instead of spending hours copying pages to share with a distant relative, a GEDCOM file can be created, saving selected data within seconds. A GEDCOM file (GEnealogical Data COMmunications) is a text file that organizes genealogical data into charts and forms that can then be shared with other computer genealogical programs. A GEDCOM file can even be transferred over the Internet, saving time and money.

Your GEDCOM of specially selected information can then be shared with other researchers and index programs. The computer genealogy program you choose to use will give you personalized directions on how to create and share a GEDCOM file. You can then post your information to be shared on forums, mailing lists, geographical sites and other genealogical web sites.

For the really adventurous researcher, you can even create your own genealogical web site and advertise your site on the Add Me Site Submission at www.addme.com/submission.htm ,which will list your web site on over a dozen search engines for free. For designing our own website check out: Yahoo!'s World Wide Web beginner's guides at dir. yahoo.com/computers_and_Internet/Internet/world/wide_web/ beginner_s_Guides.

Or simply hire someone to do it so you can spend more time researching your family history!

It is important to give back to the genealogy community and share what you have found. USGenWeb is such a wonderful resource for information, and also provides opportunities where you can be of service to others. There are so many interesting and helpful projects that you and your family could get involved with. Here are a few more ideas we thought you could try:

+ Talk to your local schools or your children's teachers to encourage them to offer a unit on genealogy. Offer to host an essay contest for the students to write about the importance of family history or some other genealogy-related topic. Most local venders will be happy to donate prizes for winners if you just ask them. Alex Haley had this to say about the value of family history to elementary students: "Family history moves students because it gives them a sense of self, a sense of dignity, a sense of worth and a sense of belonging. It helps them understand who they are."

+ Scrapbook stores are always holding special events for their customers. Offer to teach a class about preserving old photographs or how to display pedigree charts in a creative way.

+ Encourage your church to host a genealogy seminar, workshop, or conference. Invite special guest speakers who could teach others about various aspects of doing family history research.

- Once you feel comfortable in the genealogy section of your local library or Family History Center, volunteer yourself and share your knowledge with others who are just getting started.
- If you have researched a specific area or name, offer to share your expertise by hosting a Yahoo group on the Internet. They're free and easy to set up.
- Become certified as a Boy Scout Merit Counselor so you can teach classes about family history and help the boys earn their Genealogy Merit Badge! Go to www.bsa.org for more information or talk to a leader in your local Troop to find out how to get involved.
- Volunteer to serve as a docent tour guide if there is a museum or historical center in your area.
- The next time you go to the library to do genealogy, bring along a friend who would like to learn how to search for her roots too!
- Get involved in the USGenWeb Tombstone Project as a family. You can record tombstone data in a cemetery near where you live and submit it online so that other genealogists far away can have access to that data. To learn more about how you can join this important and worthwhile project go to http://www.rootsweb.com/~cemetery/

Genealogists get a ticket straight to heaven, no doubt, surrounded by all of their grateful ancestors. Genealogists who help others find what they're looking for get to go to the front of the line and eat the first bite of cake! (What's heaven without cake, after all?)

Here are some inspiring examples of some of those angel researchers who take time out of their own work to help others.

Earth Angel

by Carolyn Strickland Smalley

I don't know if you would consider me a genealogist. I'm just a country girl who goes to cemeteries and posts the information I find on the gravesites to the Internet. I am consumed by it. My husband and I want so very badly to get the information on gravesites to those who are seeking it. We try to find every grave that we can, copy down the information, and post it to the surname mailing lists on Roots Web.

I don't know how many we have posted already, but it is so rewarding to get messages back from those who are so grateful for what we've done! We're trying to get the information where it belongs—with family! We plan to keep doing this as long as we can. I've always loved family history, and I get worse day by day, I think!

Genealogy and Genetics

by Cidney Engberg
Wheaton, Illinois

The relatives on my husband's side of the family are Norwegian, Swedish and a Finlander. I proceeded to work on his mother's Norwegian side, of course, after all the elders died who could tell me anything! Never fails! I recalled my husband's aunt telling a short family story about Lars and Nils Torgelstveit, who came from Norway. They were brothers and they changed their surname to Nelson. I proved half that story to be true.

Lars "Torgilstveit" Nelson, (his real name is Törbjornsen) came from the Torgelstveit farm in Hordaland, Strandbarm. I never *could have found this location without the help of the Norway mailing list on the Internet!*

According to the story, there was supposed to be a Nils that immigrated to America. The only Nils I could find was his brother, but he stayed and worked the farm in Norway. So who was this brother that came with Lars? In the meantime, the mailing list connected me to a relative in Norway who had done a lot of work on his wife's family.

After looking at the census where Lars lived, Montana then Iowa, I never could find anyone else with the last name of Nelson from Norway. Then, the relative in Norway answered my question: Lars had an older brother named Gitle, who immigrated about 4-5 years before him. He went right to Iowa, the same place Lars finally settled after his first wife's death.

However, Gitle threw a curveball; he never changed his name to Nelson. He used the last part of the farm name, Tveit! I just wonder how they got Nels into the story. I think Gitle was hard to pronounce so they substituted Nils. So a simple little family story helped me along the way to find the ancestors.

But this story took on an odd twist that I call the "Rasmussen syndrome." Lars Nelson's first wife was Edverda Reinertsdatter. She was from Egersoya Norway, and she used her grandfather's last name of Rasmussen when she immigrated. They lived in Montana and had 3 children, although one of them died at birth. Edverda was pregnant again and suddenly, at age 38, died of a brain hemorrhage in 1916. Amazingly, the brother also died at age 38 from a brain hemorrhage. In 1976 my husband's sister died of a brain hemorrhage at age 37. I discovered that out of all of Edverda's brothers and sisters who stayed in Norway, one sister died about age 39. I suddenly started seeing a terrible trend. I have encouraged my sons to have a brain scan and to learn more about the causes of brain hemorrhages. I also told my husband's relatives to do the same. Maybe genealogy will save their lives.

The Right Place at the Right Time

by Anne Acree
Alpharetta, Georgia

In the summer of 1998, my father and mother planned to attend a 50-year reunion at their elementary school in Rochester, New York. My mother and I agreed that it would be a great opportunity to research some family history as well, so I accompanied them.

About one year earlier my mother became interested in all aspects of family history and was particularly interested in knowing more about her maternal grandmother, who had died just before my mother had married. My mother had always heard her grandmother's name as "Lydia Sheski" but when we received a copy of the marriage license the spelling of Lydia's last name was "Scheske." Where was she from? What was her correct surname? Did she have anyone else in her family? We knew only some sketchy information about her and thought she might have had a sister. Lydia's only two children were my grandmother and my great-uncle.

My mother had her grandmother in her thoughts quite regularly and then on February 8th she said she felt particularly close to her. During that night, she suddenly awakened with a flood of names and places pouring into her mind. Soon afterwards, my mother contacted her only uncle and asked if he had any other information about his mother. He mentioned that one time he remembered hearing the name "Lobuscheske," and that a "Laura Scollins" was his mother's sister.

Armed with some new leads, we headed to the town of Seneca Falls that summer, in addition to the class reunion. We located the Historical Society and went immediately to the tiny library room inside the Victorian house. It was jam-packed full of town directories, maps and local history volumes. We spent a good deal of time looking at cemetery records, directories and the like, but could not find "Scheske" anywhere. We were discussing the possibility of searching for some of the other names my mother had remembered such as "Scollins" when a library volunteer looked up. She had been silently sitting off to one side of the room, filing some papers, when suddenly she said "Did you say 'Scollins'?' This letter we just received is requesting information on 'Scollins' as well! Would you like to see it?"

The letter contained information about "Laura Lobuschefsky Scollins." That very letter was the key that lead us to learn more about Lydia, her siblings (there were many) and her parents, Charles Lobuschefsky and Anna Scholtz Lobuschefsky, immigrants to America from Germany in the 1870s! How wonderful that a helpful librarian was there to eavesdrop!

That's Czech to Me!

by Carol Willis
Colorado Springs, Colorado

My grandparents came to America from, what is now, the Czech Republic just before WWI. Grandpa had his brothers and a sister already here, but Grandma's family was still in the Czech Lands. He wouldn't permit her to say goodbye to them, fearing that she would change her mind and refuse to go with him to America.

Once they arrived here, the war broke out. Later came the Depression. Then, Grandpa died, leaving Grandma with four children and speaking very little English. Then came WWII. Well, needless to say, she never saw any of her family again.

Grandma and her mother and brothers and sisters carried on correspondence that filled the years between 1918 and the early 1950's. Grandma kept all the letters and photos. The problem is that the letters were all written in the Czech language, and none of her children or grandchildren were able to read them.

About five years ago my cousin, Darlene in Lima Ohio, told me that her mother had the letters. I told her that if she would make copies of them, I would see if I could find someone in my area to translate them. She did, and I found Olga, a woman of 90, who was born Czech and was not only bi-lingual, but was also old enough to understand the idioms of the speech of that age. There were quite a few letters and Olga and I spent many hours together. She would read them, translating into English, and I would write them out longhand, then take them home and type them. From time to time I would send the translations to Darlene, and she would share them with other family members in Ohio. As the stories unfolded, we were all astonished and saddened at the hardships they endured and the hope that they would be together again, hope that gradually, but never entirely, faded.

Once Olga and I completed the task of translating and transcribing the letters, I began to wonder if any family member might still be left in the Czech Republic, not of the earlier generation, of course, but some living relative. But where to begin? The Prochazka's (Grandmother's family) seemed to move all over, and no letter or postcard bore a stamp from the same location. I decided to join the Czech-American Genealogy Society (a national group) because I knew they had telephone directories of all the towns and villages in the Czech Republic, and would look up names and addresses for members.

I blindly selected a postcard from Kralupy (a small town south of Prague) and asked them to provide me with a dozen addresses for people there with the last name of Prochazka. (I will tell you that it is a very common name.)

When the list arrived I saw that no one had a first name that was familiar, so I again, blindly, selected two names. I asked Olga to help me construct a letter in Czech, asking if we could be related, and included copies of family photos that they might have in their own family albums, if indeed we were related. My idea was to begin with these two and then move on to other names and then other towns as I searched.

I sent off the letter and photo packets and waited. After a few weeks I received a letter from a very surprised gentleman. It turned out that his grandfather and my grandmother were brother and sister!!! The other letter I sent had gone to his brother!!! We have since continued a correspondence, and he has been able to "fill in some blanks" for us. Eventually I want to go there and meet them for myself.

Darlene is sure, and so am I, that it was Grandmother, herself, who orchestrated the whole thing. Surely her hand was in it, how else could we possibly have found family after all the years?

Sweet Dreams

by Ron Bremer
Paradise, Utah

A genealogy instructor was a house-guest of one of the ladies who had attended his seminar earlier in the day. He relates that after dinner his hostess said, "May I ask you a question about my grandfather, Henry Gabelbauer?" She then described in great detail all the research she had done on this German ancestor who had immigrated to Milwaukee, Wisconsin. For all her diligent searching she kept hitting brick walls and couldn't find the information she wanted so desperately. She had hoped her guest could offer some ideas. He gladly provided several suggestions for research tips.

The next morning he began a polite conversation by asking her how she had slept. She surprised him with her reply, "I did not sleep a wink all night. After I went to bed, my grandfather appeared in my room at the foot of my bed and spent the night telling me why I could not find his genealogy records." Then she said, "I now know exactly where to search for his information and I am thrilled to death!" And so she did.

CHAPTER ASSIGNMENT:

Begin to collect vital statistic documents on the ancestor of your choice. Ultimately, collect and organize records for all four sets of your grandparents. Organize them into files with each married couple as parents by the paternal surname and then file them alphabetically. Post their information online to share.

CHAPTER 10

Caring For Seedlings

Family reunions and nurturing relationships with living relatives

Did you know that October is National Family History month? For a true genealogist, every month celebrates families and any day is a good reason to champion the cause of family heritage! National Family History month is a great opportunity for all of us to evaluate how our research is going and to celebrate our discoveries with our families. Teaching your family to know and cherish your unique heritage is a great gift you can give to your loved ones. There is strength in roots. It's especially important to pass on a love for your family's legacy to your children. Someone once said, "A family tree can wither if nobody tends its roots."

One mother shared her humbling realization, "I would find myself resenting the constant demands of my young children while I tried to work on my family history for just an hour or two each week. It finally dawned on me that I was teaching my children to resent genealogy, because I was frequently pushing them away. Instead, I now try to conscientiously stop and tell them about the ancestor I'm researching and how they're related. Sometimes I just need to stop and remember that they're alive and need my attention now! Our deceased ancestors will always be there to research, but my kids won't always be small children."

There are so many creative things that families can do to celebrate their heritage and participate in the spirit of National Family History month. Be sure to check out all of the fun activity ideas for families in Chapter 6, as well as the creative craft and décor projects in Chapter 8! They can help make "dead" history become alive for you and your loved ones all year long! Create some memories to preserve for your own family. In other words, put down the genealogy books and go out and play! (Don't forget to pick up the research again, later though!)

A fun way to keep family history on the minds of your relatives is to send them a "Genealogy Bumper Sticker" or "Thought for the Day" via e-mail during the month of October (or for as long as they'll put up with it!) Here are a few to get you started:

- My ancestors must be in a Genealogy Witness Protection Plan.
- Shake your family tree and watch the nuts fall out!
- How can one ancestor cause so much trouble?
- I looked into my family tree and found out I was a sap.
- If only people came with pull-down menus and online help.
- Isn't Genealogy Fun? The answer to one problem leads to two more.
- After 30 days, unclaimed ancestors will be adopted.
- Genealogists are Time Unravelers.
- Genealogy—tracing yourself back to better people.

- A pack-rat is hard to live with, but makes a great ancestor.
- Genealogists' last words: "I should have asked them before they died."
- My family is always late. My ancestors arrived on the June Flower.
- SHH!! Be very, very quiet, I'm hunting forebears.
- Genealogists live life in the Past Lane.
- Cousins marrying cousins : Very Tangled Roots.
- Genealogy - Chasing your own tale!
- I searched my family tree and apparently I don't exist.
- Genealogy is not fatal, but it is a grave disease.
- Old Genealogists never die—they just lose their census.
- SOOOOO Many Ancestors—So little time!
- There is strength in roots.
- Genealogists always do the write thing.
- Genealogists will never leave you in the dust.

Nurturing relationships with family members who are still alive is a great benefit of doing family history research. A wonderful idea is to create a "Sibling Book." Each book or binder focuses on just one sibling and is created to let that person know how much he is loved and what a great blessing he has been to the family. Gather pictures of him from when he was a baby, youth and adult. Have family members fill out papers that begin with open-ended questions such as:

- My life has been blessed by you because...
- Your best talents and qualities are...
- The things I most admire about you are...

+ My greatest memories of you are when…
+ A funny experience I shared with you once was when…
+ You made a difference in my life by…
+ Some of the things I have learned from you are…

Can you imagine receiving a book filled with pages like that from your family? What a treasured keepsake that would be!

A similar idea can be used to create a special book for someone's birthday or anniversary, especially for a landmark year such as 25 or 50. Ask family and friends of the guest of honor to write letter of congratulations, highlighting memories, stories, and reflections of their time together. Encourage them to include photos which personalize their letter even more. Gather all of the letters in a special binder and present them on the special day. What a fun way to see a life through the eyes of those who have shared it!

The wonderful blessing of e-mail has brought us all closer to our loved ones and even to relatives we never knew we had, but there is still no substitute for getting together in person. Even the best-written letter can't compare with sitting down next to Uncle Alvin and laughing together about the story of when he tricked Aunt Darla into smashing the butter with her bare hands at Thanksgiving. Do you really want to wait until a funeral to get the whole clan together? It's time for a family reunion! Throw in some sight-seeing and entertainment and you've got yourself a real family vacation!

Family reunions have been a great summer tradition for many families. You can have a small get-together of your closest relatives or a great bash for everyone you can find dangling from your family tree. Sure, it can be a lot of work, but all things worthwhile are. Besides, as a genealogist, a reunion can be one of your finest moments where you can not only show off all your hard work, but also gather even more information!

Once a party is announced, relatives usually get very excited and want to make sure that their research and family line is being represented. The more people that are involved in the planning, the more enthusiasm and better attendance you will find. Surround yourself with a team of dedicated helpers and start as much as a year in advance.

There are tons of great resources in books as well as on Internet that can walk you step by step from planning the event to the final clean-up when it's over. For a jumpstart, check out the following web sites:

+ www.familyreunion.com
+ www.familyfun.com
+ www.familysearch.com/reunions
+ www.family-reunion.com
+ http://genealogy.about.com/od/family_reunions/
+ www.reunionindex.com
+ www.reuniontips.com

One of the first tasks in planning a family reunion is to send out a letter to all of the relatives as far up the family tree you think you'd like to go in order to solicit suggestions and volunteers. It's helpful to write out a time-line to keep you from feeling overwhelmed that you have to do everything at once. Be sure to keep a reunion notebook so you can keep track of who you have delegated tasks to such as menu planning, activities, lodging, entertainment and so forth.

You can't hold a reunion without guests, so be sure to pick a date and location that work well for everyone. Let everyone know as far in advance as possible so they can both make arrangements for the event in their schedule and enjoy the anticipation! You'll also need to decide how the reunion will be paid for. There are many ways to share costs such as setting a registration fee, asking relatives to donate supplies and services, and even setting up a reunion scholarship fund. A fun idea is to hold an auction where people can get rid of their "white elephant" junk, sell handmade crafts and culinary masterpieces. Money earned from the auction could fund the meat and drinks, while everyone else brings a side dish or dessert to share.

Be sure to encourage everyone to bring memorabilia to display on a designated table. Prepare some special awards to present to whomever traveled the farthest or has the most children or create some goofy awards for the sexiest grandma or the uncle with the hairiest legs. Don't forget a prize for the family members who look most like a particular ancestor. Some families choose a fun theme for their reunion based on their ancestors' heritage, occupation, or location. Using a theme ties all aspects of the event together, making it easier to design everything from the invitations and decorations to the food and even activities. Here are just a few ideas for fun themes to try at your next family gathering:

- "Home-Spun Fun" (Country Fair, cooking contests, pets, clogging)
- "Home Matters" (Construction motif, building relationships)
- "From My House To Yours" (Use rows of houses with different architecture that reflects the personalities of the families)
- "Hearts Knit In Harmony" (Hearts, music, knitting service project)
- "Roots and Branches" (Trees, garden)

- "Family Times" (Newspaper, breaking news, reporters, show family videos, CNN-style)
- "Love Bears All Things" (We can bearly think of any ideas here)
- "Angels Among Us" (Someone has to bring the angel food cake!)
- "Survivors" (Island motif based on the reality TV show "Survivor")
- "Christmas in July" (Think stockings, caroling, elf caps, and Christmas cookies)
- "Luau" (Who doesn't love seeing Uncle Randy in a grass skirt?)
- "Olympics Unplugged" (Games, torches, country flags, opening and closing ceremonies)
- "Family Circus" (Things under the red top or that cute family cartoon of the same name)
- "Mexican Fiesta" (Even better if your family has some Hispanic heritage!)
- "Family History Under The Sea" (Seafood, water games, ocean décor)

Living History

by Janet Graham Theberge
Fredericksburg, Texas

I've always loved hearing my parents and grandparents tell stories. As I sat, legs dangling under a chair, listening to family stories, I learned to love the things they did and the way they lived. It seemed strange that things were so different for them than they were for me. The stories never failed to bring me in from outdoor adventures. They were far better than the make-believe world I shared outside with my brothers and sister.

The lives of the people my History teachers taught me about were only vaguely interesting, nothing to get very excited about. Then one day, when I was talking with my grandmother (98 years young), it dawned on me that I had been learning and loving history all my life. I had just never connected those wonderful family stories with the events and people my History teachers had been talking about when I was in school. Wow! The world of the past suddenly opened up for me! I connected everything I learned to something I had learned from my parents or grandparents. It all fit into place, and it was all so fascinating!

Later on, in my adult years, my father took on a project that he believed was important enough to devote years of effort to – our family genealogy. He visited libraries, newspaper offices, courthouses, and churches. He met relatives he had never known, and he wrote (and received) hundreds of letters. When he visited older relatives, he always took along a tape recorder so that he could record their memories. Many of them pulled out old trunks and photo albums to show him things they had. He acquired thousands of photos of family members as well as old documents relating to our family's history.

I was very much interested in Daddy's project. Every time he found something new he shared it with me, so I came to understand his devotion to the "cause". One evening as we were pouring over some original land grants that had been given to Daddy, he confided his reason for taking on the family genealogy, "Nobody is keeping our family's history alive. I have seen my dad, and my aunts and uncles die off, and in just a few years nobody will know they lived. They might know they EXISTED, but they won't know how they LIVED. I want them to be just as alive to your grandchildren as they were to me." That clinched it for me.

I took over the job of the family genealogist, and I enjoy telling my children the stories I heard as a child. I now have two grandchildren who are too young to understand what I do, but someday I hope they will appreciate my work, and if they don't, that's OK, too. Somewhere there will be a library full of the work my father and I have done so that the next family researcher won't have to dig quite so deep.

My Brother, the Stranger

by Jim Bates
Australia

This happened before I was 'up to my eyeballs' in family history, a forewarning, or something like that! I was working at the de Havilland Engine Company in Edgware as an engine build inspector at the end of World War II. The floor laborer was Ernie Witherspoon. The Chief Inspector sent for me and said they had looked through the files and noted that I had previous experience working with gears. The Gear Inspector was being promoted to a new position, leaving a vacancy in a job I was interested in. The next day I worked in the factory next door and took up the duties of a gear inspector. My very first task was to give the okay to another employee on a gear blank so that he could go ahead and finish the batch. I checked it to the drawing, found it ok, and stamped it with my inspection stamp. When I started to enter the details in my day book I asked him his name.

"John Witherspoon."

"Oh! You have a brother working in the factory?"

"No brothers or sisters."

"Oh. Where do you hail from?"

"A little place you've never heard of, Great Snoring in Essex."

"Thanks John."

I gave him back his stamped sample and he went back to his lathe. I looked around, but because nobody seemed to be needing my attention I walked back to my old factory.

I walked right up to Ernie, who was sweeping the floor and said, "Ernie, as a matter of interest, where do you hail from?"

"Oh, a little place you've never heard of, Little Snoring in Essex."

"And how far is Little Snoring from Great Snoring?"

"About three miles."

"If you're not doing anything special right now, come for a walk with me."

He looked at me very suspiciously. "What's up?" he asked.

"Just hush and come for a walk."

We walked into the workshop past my new work station and up to the lathe where John was working. He saw us coming, switched off his lathe, and stepped out on to the gangway, "What crime have I committed?" he joked.

"No crime. John Witherspoon of Great Snoring meet Ernie Witherspoon of Little Snoring."

I left them staring at one another with their mouths wide open while I went back to my work station. They both came and thanked me—they were half brothers—and neither knew that the other existed!

P.S. WITHERSPOON is a substitute surname, but the places are true!

Converted To Genealogy

by J. Wren Harris, Jr.
Albany, Georgia

Dad was always interested in the origins of his family, but he didn't have time to do any serious research until he was able to retire in 1982. After he retired, he started visiting libraries and courthouses and corresponding with others who were doing research on our family lines. He would talk about what he had learned about our family's ancestors, where they had lived, and what had happened to them. I enjoyed listening to him, but I have to admit that I wasn't interested enough to get involved.

When Dad died in 1985, part of the work that I did to help settle his affairs was to go through his genealogy files. I looked through the family folders and the pedigree charts and saw some of the family names and locations that he had talked about. I still wasn't interested in continuing the research, so I put it all away.

Then, in June 1988, my son applied for his first appointment as a Methodist minister. He was assigned a circuit of three small churches in the middle of Georgia. Two of these churches were in the towns of Irwinton and Toomsboro in Wilkinson County, Georgia. The third church, named Salem, was also in Wilkinson County, but was located out in the country. We visited the churches in the towns first and then went to find Salem. We found it on a dirt road and saw that it was a small wooden church, painted white, well cared for, with an old cemetery beside it. We walked among the graves, reading the inscriptions. The names Wynn and Thompson on several of the tombstones seemed faintly familiar to me, but I couldn't really place them. We wrote down as many of the names and dates as we could make out on the old, worn stones. When we got home, I pulled out Dad's old genealogy files and found that among the people buried there were my great-great-grandparents, James Russell Thompson and his wife, the former Martha Patricia Wynn! Several members of their families were also buried at that cemetery. They were all early members of the Salem Methodist Church – the very same church where my son was to begin his ministry!

I wanted to find out more about these ancestors. Who were they? Where did they live? Where did they come from? What was it like when they were alive?

I began doing research to find answers to these questions, and at some point, I realized that I had become hooked on this thing called genealogy. I'm still hooked. I discovered that genealogy is a jigsaw puzzle that you can never finish because there are no borders and you keep finding more pieces. It's a never-ending story full of brave and wonderful people (and a few scoundrels) who lived, worked, and raised families in circumstances that we can only try to imagine.

It is history that grabs you, because it is your very own family that was involved when the history was actually happening. And hopefully, it's a legacy that we can leave for people not yet born.

Family Heirlooms

Caring for seedlings can also mean caring for material objects. Sometimes, as we anxiously climb trees, we climb the wrong one. Finding special relics and treasures shouldn't be discarded simply because they don't pertain to your own family line. The Internet is a wonderful resource that can be used to help finders locate the true

owners of family heirlooms. Be sure to visit the following websites:
www.honoringourancestors.com/orphanphotos.html
www.lostandfound@tias.com
www.deadfred.com
www.ancientfaces.com
www.yourpastconnections.com
www.petuniapress.com
www.heirloomslost.com
www.pastvoices.com
www.idreamof.com/lost.html

Like most of the sites above, the Tias website publishes information about generous people who have found items belonging to other people's families so they can be reunited with the proper owners or their descendents. They accept three types of "lost and found" submissions for publication in their newsletter.

1. You have a vintage item in hand and you are trying to find relatives of the original owner. This could be an old photo album, baby book, diploma, Family Bible, or other vintage items that can be linked to a specific person or family.
2. You are looking for a fairly common vintage item that has deep personal meaning for you or someone you know.
3. If you have a friend or relative that has been lost for at least 10 years, the website can help you locate missing persons.

Recently, a man was casually looking in an antique store, when the owner welcomed him to the store and casually asked his name. When the store owner learned the customer's name, he opened a drawer in his desk and said, "Here, I have something for you." It was an old newspaper article with a picture of the very same customer when he was a young boy with a group from his grammar school. The store owner had held onto that article for just that moment. He knew sooner or later he would meet someone in that class who would treasure the photo!

Finding someone else's family history

by Karen Glockel
Bellevue, Nebraska

I love genealogy, but every once in awhile I take a break from it and roam through the antique stores (a second love of mine.) On this particular day it was bright and sunny, just right for a car ride to an antique mall that is about 20 miles or so away from my home. Usually I just go to the stores nearest to my downtown area, but getting on the interstate and driving sounded good to me on this day.

I walked up and down the isles of the large antique mall, not looking for anything in particular. One booth caught my eye, as it sold glass and china, so I stopped. I am not sure why, but I happened to glance under the table and saw a basket with some old, beautifully framed documents of baptisms, confirmations, etc. I recognized one of the names because it was an unusual one. I really thought that it couldn't possibly belong to the family I believed it did. The last name was Rezak, the same name as my daughter's 5th grade teacher in school that year. The framed document was not expensive, so I bought it, not knowing if it belonged to the Rezak family I knew.

    I brought it home and told my daughter to ask her teacher if she knew the male Rezak name on the document. My daughter returned from school the next day and told me that her teacher was convinced it was her husband's grandfather! I could not believe it! I delivered the beautiful record the next day to a very grateful Mrs. Rezak. After giving it to her, I had a gnawing feeling that I should go back to the antique mall. So that very day, I retuned to the mall, went to the same booth I had found the Rezak document and looked beneath the table again through the baskets of things. I once again found another item with the Rezak name on it! It was a beautifully framed wedding certificate. I couldn't believe it. Neither could Mrs. Rezak! The Rezaks were grateful for the lost pieces of their heritage and gave our family a night out on the town, which the kids especially enjoyed. Mrs. Rezak went that next weekend to the antique mall, but did not find any more family treasures in that booth. They still do not know how those precious family documents got out of the family. I was glad I could find someone else's family history.

CHAPTER ASSIGNMENT:

Make a list of all the living relatives you have lost touch with and decide how you will locate them. Recruit the help of another relative who can help you create a database that can be shared with all of your family.

CHAPTER 11

Seeing The Forest Through The Trees

The Nature of Family History...Taking A Step Back To See Clearer

Sometimes after having your head buried intensely in a book you can forget that you're sitting in a beautiful park with a duck pond and blooming spring flowers all around! Genealogy can be like that! Sometimes, it's beneficial to pull back from the intensity of the task you may be pursuing and change your perspective and view. It may just be enlightening to see things in a different light.

Enlightened by the Dark

by Jerry Levan
York, Pennsylvania

I am an amateur genealogist doing research on my family ancestry. I often help others who can not travel to York, Pennsylvania to get information or copies. One such person is a lady from Springfield Illinois. She had been looking for the parents of two children, her ancestors.

I took it upon myself to try and help her find the parents of Emanuel and Lydia Bates. I visited the burial ground of Emanuel Bates and was hoping to find "Son of..." on his marker, but did not. On the tombstone record, provided me by the cemetery, there were eight plots,

but only six were indicated as being used. I was hoping to find other markers in the plot that could be for his parents. I discovered two very old markers which could not be read at all and two little markers. I identified the little markers as being those of two young children of Emanuel and his wife Sarah. The markers were in a very poor state and I could not read them either. The other two markers were easily read and I began taking notes.

I had brought along my five year old daughter Madeleine with me. I expected to be there only about ten minutes, however, Madeleine was full of questions. It was getting late and the sun was going down. A full moon was now clearly visible in the eastern sky. She remained persistent in her questioning and wanted to know about the little ones "over there," pointing. She wanted to see the markers of the little ones. It became twilight. I sat her down on one of the four family boundary markers, a big square concrete B. The ground was very wet and slippery and she stayed where I placed her. I took down information on the other markers, all the while fielding her questions.

She still wanted to see the markers of the little ones. She was full of excitement and play. I told her to stay where she was so as not to get her feet wet. I would only be a minute longer. Well, curiosity got the best of her and off she went to the markers. I finished and went over to collect her, when I realized I could now read some of the little markers. As I sat there, trying to speculate what was carved into the sandstone, the inscriptions revealed themselves in the growing shadows of the approaching darkness. They were two little boys. Hammond was ten and his brother's stone, the only one Madeleine wanted to touch, was Willie's. He was also five years old. Twilight had helped me see what could not be seen in daylight.

My little granddaughter had also helped me find the hidden grave for this couple. I have since dispatched the information off to Springfield, Illinois. It solved a few riddles and filled in a few holes for her. I felt very sad when I initially saw the little markers, but later I felt happy and privileged.

A byproduct of doing genealogy is to learn the nature of people. It's not very often when you discover that your ancestors were famous people who accomplished notable feats. More often than not, you learn that your ancestors were just ordinary people, courageously facing life's daily challenges, which in itself is worth adulation. It is said "Circumstances don't make the man, they reveal the man." A genealogist's task is to learn all the circumstances surrounding a person's life that reveals him or her to his family.

Shakespeare's Neighbors

by Tera Bates Duncan
Cedar Hills, Utah

When my husband and I took a trip to Europe in 2002, I wanted to make the traveling worthwhile, so I prepared my ancestors' names by categorizing them into location of birth. I made a list of all those born in Paris, France, Munich, Germany, Interlaken, Switzerland, and several towns in England.

Whenever we visited a city where some of my ancestors were

born, I would go to that city's library and cemetery to look for their names. We had visited several countries without much luck finding the ancestors I was looking for.

When we went to Stratford, England, I had one family, named Rogers, on my direct line whose members were born there in the early 1600s. When I visited the church where William Shakespeare was buried, a powerful feeling came over me that this Rogers family was buried in that same cemetery. I felt that the spirit of Elijah was blessing me with quite a profound experience in order to teach me that my Rogers ancestors know me and are grateful for the efforts I have made in their behalf.

I looked at all the gravestones and found that they were contemporaries of William Shakespeare, even neighbors of his family in the mid 1600's! I pictured myself as part of the Rogers family, walking the streets, and participating in history as they lived their daily lives.

The sense of peace I felt while in that cemetery gave me the motivation I needed to continue work on the Rogers line. Now I want to find their parents and grandparents. The experience was a highlight of the memories I now have of Europe and my ancestry there.

High School History Was Never This Much Fun!

by Sandra Riggins
Carlsbad, California

The thing that I've found the most fun about doing genealogy is seeing history come alive through my family tree. More than fifteen years ago I found out that I had ancestors who lived in Salem

Massachusetts during the time of the witch trials. I rushed off to get library books to see if my family were the witches or the accusers. Although it appears that my family was neutral, at least as far as all the recorded events are concerned I found studying the time period great fun.

As I continue to research and get farther back in history each time period comes alive to me. Each of these eras that I paid only half attention to in school is alive because I feel like I'm personally acquainted with someone who lived through it.

One of the most special family history events had to do with recent history. I was visiting my parents a few years after my grandmother had passed away and my mother showed me a box of letters that my grandmother had saved. In it were all the letters she had received from my father while he was serving in WWII. I borrowed them and transcribed them into a book for him which I gave as a gift one Father's Day. I've always known my father as someone 30 years my senior but to read his letters written when he was a very young man put a new face on the Father that I love. It was amazing how the story opened up to me as I typed each of those letters in order. I vicariously worried with him and my Grandmother as I typed the letters about how he was being sent to the front lines. How vivid war became to me as he described living the winter in a fox hole! How relieved I was to read the letter stating that he was back off the front lines.

Despite the fact that I knew the ending, it was a remarkable story and kept me spellbound. I developed a greater appreciation for my father and for my grandmother who had her two sons serving in the military during WWII including one in a prisoner of war camp. I also gained greater appreciation for our great country and the *sacrifices made by those who have served throughout the years to keep the country free and allow me to live the way I do.*

Tracey feels a true kinship to her great-great-grandfather, as she explains in the following sory:

Visiting With My Favorite Relative

The nature of genealogy truly is spiritual. One of my favorite relatives that I like to visit with isn't even alive! I have a personal relationship with my great-great-grandfather, whom I have never met. By researching his family and his descendants, I have spent many hours looking for him in documents.

I feel a particular fondness towards him due to the warmth and peace that envelopes me whenever I'm researching his life. Like many genealogists, I often have quiet internal conversations with the person I'm hunting for at the time.

Often I'll say, "Where in the world are you? How come you aren't in that census where I thought you'd be?"

And then I hear whispers to my soul. "I moved out of the state sweetheart," or "Don't forget all of my children."

The most overwhelming message I have received from this great grandfather is that he loves me more than I even know. He is more aware of me and his grandchildren than I realize. It is his family and his posterity that he still cares about.

If there are guardian angels in the heavens appointed to watch over us, I believe it will be by our own ancestors and not by strangers.

CHAPTER ASSIGNMENT:

Complete family group sheets for your 4 grandparents as children and parents. This will generate 8 more family group sheets, which lists your aunts and uncles. This will then develop into over a dozen or more as you continue to list all their children as parents!

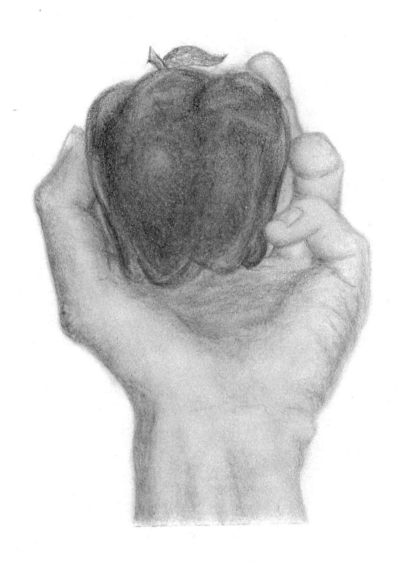

Tasting The Fruit Of The Tree

Enjoying the fruits of our labors

It would be very fulfilling to complete your pedigree all the way back to Adam and Eve.

Actually we, the authors, can claim that! Well ok, we confess…we can show that our pedigree goes to an Adam and Eve Derryberry, of Burke County, North Carolina in 1740!

We always chuckle when someone smugly claims "all my genealogy is done." Usually the claim is followed by the clarification that some distant aunt did it all. As extensive as some pedigrees may be, there is still always more to do and not enough hours in one lifetime to do it all. If someone else did all your genealogy, frankly, you'd miss out on all the fun and adventure! All the records that you will research and families you will find will be a precious gift to yourself.

One friend enjoyed the honor and title of "Family Genealogist" until she realized there was no reason to hoard all the family records and she could use some help researching all the names! Combining efforts and delegating research projects with her family members became a unifying force. By carefully preserving and organizing your family tree you can enjoy the fruits of the tree together for many generations. Your work will be added upon by future generations which will see the rings on the tree enlarge.

Cousins, Friends And Kindred Spirits

by Renné Harrington Blocker
Manlius, New York

It has always been my belief that God puts people in our paths at different times in our life for various reasons. People are placed on our path to walk the road of life with us, sometimes for a short while, and sometimes for a lifetime. Doing genealogy has heightened this belief for me.

I began to search for my family roots exactly three years ago. For Easter, my husband gave me a laptop computer and a disk for creating your family tree. This intrigued me, as my father and everyone else in his family died in their forties. I knew virtually nothing about the ancestors that shared my surname and there wasn't a living person to ask about my heritage.

My curiosity about my ancestors got the best of me and I ran a search on the Internet for genealogy websites. The very first thing I did was place a query on a genealogy website. The only thing I knew about my grandparents was where they originally came from. I placed a query, asking if anyone had any information about my relatives. Almost immediately I received an answer back from someone who had a complete family tree on my ancestors. I had found a relative with one click! "Wow, this genealogy thing is going to be really easy," I thought to myself. Of course, all of you reading this are laughing to yourselves, as you know it wasn't long before "SPLAT!" I ran into one of those proverbial brick walls.

I soon found out that the gentleman who answered the query was my third cousin. We swapped family stories, phone numbers, e-mail and home addresses. We promised to keep each other abreast of any developments in our mutual search for our family roots. It was almost as if there was some type of magnetic force we had stumbled upon, because within eleven days another "cousin" answered my query. Oddly enough, this new cousin lives only 20 miles from the third cousin I had just come in contact with eleven days previously! Neither gentleman knew of one another's existence.

Within a very short period of time, the three of us joined forces in our search. We combined efforts and swapped Bible pages, pictures, birth and death certificates and family stories. Both of my new found cousins were in the military and we all were in awe when we found out that our 2nd great grand uncle was killed in battle during the Civil War. His body was never recovered and there was never even a marker to commemorate that he had served and died for his country. One of my proudest accomplishments is that I was able to get a Civil War marker placed next to his mother's headstone. I filled out an application with the Veterans Affairs and now the world can see that our relative was a Sergeant, served in the Civil War, and was killed in battle. Two hundred and forty years after his death, he is now at peace.

In the three years I have been doing my research, my database has grown to nearly 1,300 relatives. I have had cousins from all over America come and stay at my home and go to my county's public library to research their line with me. I have put branches of my husband's family in touch with each other also. The absolute best part of my searching is the friends I have found. One of my very best friends is the town historian of the town most of my ancestors hail from. She not only connected me with my ancestors, but she and I connected in a very special way. Somebody or some force definitely threw our lives together and enriched them for the better.

Through my researching, I have found generations of my family tree. This summer over three hundred of us were able to attend a cousin's wedding! We are able to keep in contact with each other and attend family reunions. I have an extensive media database and try to update pictures so that each family member has a current picture next to their name in my database. I have e-mail "group" lists and keep all branches of the family in touch with each other and informed of the latest joys and births and deaths.

Two weeks ago a first cousin of mine lost everything in a fire. She considers her greatest loss to be the pictures of her parents and other deceased family members. Everyone contributed their family pictures to my database, so now, when my cousin is ready to move into a new home I will be able to recreate all of her family pictures that were lost in the fire.

I waited two and a half years to contact one of my first cousins to ask for her family's information for my database. The reason I waited so long is that she and I had lost contact with each other about twenty years ago and I just didn't think that she would be interested in anything to do with our family history. I contacted her just six months ago and she has been a wealth of family stories, information that would have been lost forever had she not shared her memories with me. We came into each other's lives just before family crises hit both of us and we have been there for each other every step of the way. I met her grown daughter for the first time four months ago and now she and I have formed a strong bond and are inseparable.

One of my initial genealogy contacts was the second cousin who answered my original query on the genealogy board. Once our initial contact was made we have been in contact on a daily basis. If we don't e-mail each other back and forth at least three times a day, we will call each other long distance.

We are both really amazed by our relationship because there was an immediate connection, as if we had known each other all of our lives. In three years we have become best friends, confidantes and kindred spirits. We have seen each other through illness and deaths and disappointments and we will always be there for each other. The gentlemen who first answered my query has become closer to me than my brothers. We are in constant contact and he spent a recent holiday weekend here at my home. In the last few months he and I have been able to collaborate and get back to the 1700s on our main family line.

I believe that everything happens in life for a reason. My husband was meant to give me this computer with the Family Tree Maker disk. I was meant to do my genealogy. I was destined to be my family's "storyteller."

Although my family is not one of great wealth or importance, I was given the job of weaving our family's tapestry together. I have been able to bring comfort to a few people, bring families together, and even settle a 25-year family feud! Genealogy has enriched my life and the lives of my family. We all now feel connected and have a real sense of family and roots.

From Her Roots

by Sheila Huntington
Centerville, Utah

My mother died in the spring, leaving a big hole in my life. A few days after her death, a thoughtful neighbor dropped by for a visit with a gift, a framed sentiment entitled "A Mother's Roots," an excerpt from Motherless Daughters: The Legacy of Loss by Hope Edelman.

The author explains that in the Redwood ecosystem, all seeds are contained in pods called burls, tough brown clumps that grow where the mother tree's trunk and root system meet. When the mother tree is logged, blown over, or destroyed by fire, the trauma stimulates the burls' growth hormones. The seeds release, and the trees sprout around her creating a circle of daughters. The daughter trees grow by absorbing the sunlight their mother cedes to them when she dies. They get the moisture and nutrients they need from their mother's root system, which remains intact even after her leaves die. Although the daughters exist independently of their mother above ground, they continue to draw sustenance from her underneath.

Those thoughts helped me to realize that, although my mother's physical presence was gone, she lived on in her three daughters. We are physically, intellectually and spiritually a part of her. Everything we do in some way reflects her influence, her teachings, her values, even her mannerisms.

The next spring after my mother's death, we noticed that the flowering plum tree that had shaded my mother's bedroom window was diseased and dying. The tree, a key part of the front landscape, was located at the base of a gentle slope covered with St. John's

Wort. A waterfall meandered down the slope through the ground cover, past the tree and birdbath, under a bridge and finished in the pool below. In early summer, the ground- cover blossomed with beautiful yellow flowers and the waterfall played a cheery tune to accompany the birds who were attracted to the birdbath and the pink-blossomed tree. The sights and sounds of nature brought a peaceful joy to my mother's room.

Many times we are reluctant to let the things we love leave our comfortable and secure lives. As with my mother, it was time to say goodbye to this once beautiful tree. And so, reluctantly, my husband cut the tree down even with the lawn. A few weeks later we noticed a little sprout growing up through the lawn from the roots of the flowering plum tree. Soon the little sprout grew into a strong and straight tree, a daughter identical to her mother, who today blooms and shades just the way her mother did.

Our kind and merciful Father gives us these elegant metaphors to comfort and guide us. We can be grateful for the legacy of a mother's love, those inherent qualities that makes us a part of her.

CHAPTER ASSIGNMENT:

Attend or plan a family reunion on any side of your family tree. Maybe there's a regular reunion for one of your family surnames and you've never been. Commit to join up with that family this year. If you don't have anyone already organizing a family reunion, take the plunge and dive into the event by planning one yourself. Decide on a date/time/location and write your list of those to be included. It's okay if it's a small turn-out this year. Worthy traditions take time!

CHAPTER 13

Fruitful Distractions

Family Facts and Fables

Have you ever heard someone test your intelligence by claiming, "My grandfather died in the Revolutionary War years before he met my grandmother!" or "It's been genetically proven that if your grandparents didn't have any children, then you won't either." Family fables and stories are the rays of sunlight that shimmer through the leaves on your family tree. They can capture an audience of young children around a campfire and hold the attention of bored teenagers at a family reunion. More times than not, they are pure fiction, but you just might find enough truth in them to lead you to the facts.

Emotions range from those who relish in the thought of finding famous ancestry to those who shudder to find the "skeletons in the closet." Either way, they're all part of what made us who we are today. Every family tree has some sap in it! Enjoying the fables might just kindle enough curiosity in another family member so you can recruit some help with your quest for the true history of your family. Treasure your heritage, but don't take it so seriously that you can't laugh at all the nuts on your family tree.

In the form of David Letterman's famous "Top Ten," here are some ways you can tell if you're taking your genealogy research a little too seriously:

Top Ten Indicators That You Are Spending Too Much Time Doing Genealogy

10. Your favorite film of all time is the 1850 census index.
9. You hyperventilate at the sight of an old cemetery.
8. When all of your correspondence begins "You don't know me, but I think we might be related."
7. You have more photographs of dead people than living ones.
6. You ask your relatives to bring DNA samples to your family reunion.
5. You've traced every one of your ancestral lines back to Adam and Eve and still don't want to quit.
4. You marry the County Clerk so you'll have access to more records around the clock.
3. You asked Santa to bring your very own microfilm reader for Christmas.
2. You get locked in a library overnight and you never even notice.
1. You're pretty sure your ancestor has been spotted in several places with Elvis!

Mystery Solved

by Irene Fuller Oliver
La Mesa, California

My father died early at age 39. We had tried to do genealogy, but kept hitting dead ends on his line. We had only a birth-date, handwritten in the family Bible. One year after my Uncle Jim's death, my brother-in-law, Bob Kite, was sent from Texas to Ohio for Army Reserve training. He was an avid genealogist, and went to the various sources in Ohio, finding lots of information while there. He even helped us solve an old family mystery. We discovered that my grandfather was born in Germany, not in the USA, which was what was written in the family Bible! There were German schools and English schools in the area, so my grandfather wrote in the Bible that he was born in America, instead of Germany so that his kids could go to an English school! We felt that it wasn't just coincidence that Bob was sent to Ohio.

Relatives and Synchronicity

by Sherry D. Ruais
Dale City, Virginia

Last year I was surfing the Internet, looking for genealogy sites pertaining to the Jackson's of West Virginia. I happened upon a strange web site advertising a Ghost Walk. Amazingly, it was scheduled for almost the same time I had planned to be in West Virginia to do some research. I was intrigued and thought to myself "Why not do both at the same time?" I called my mother and asked her if she would like to attend the Ghost Walk events with me and she said yes. I bought tickets and made the arrangements.

When we arrived at the main building site, where the information and directions for the Ghost Events were given out, we learned it was going to be held in the local museum. The Ghost Walk area was upstairs and the museum was on the first floor. We arrived early so we walked around to look at their exhibit. Imagine my surprise when the featured exhibit was Lily Irene Jackson - a distant relative of mine!

She was an artist and they had gathered several of her works to display as their main attraction. She not only painted her numerous dogs, but also a couple of self-portraits. I was given permission to take pictures of the paintings. Among the exhibits were several photographs of her at various ages and her home. The most interesting was a reprint of a period piece about her unusual wedding. She had been, what was called in those days, a spinster, somewhat past the usual age to marry. She often painted her own calling cards and decorated them with feathers. This time she made the invitations to her own wedding. They stated that she was to marry F.H.C. on the appointed date, and they were mailed out to fifty people. The whole town was buzzing about the wedding, wondering who F.H.C. was. No one knew of any gentleman with those initials.

When the wedding ceremony began, she walked down the stairway in her beautiful gown. At the same time three friends came out of a door in the parlor carrying wreaths. On each wreath was a banner with the words Faith, Hope, and Charity on them! You see, she just wanted to get married and have some fun with her friends, so she married Faith, Hope and Charity! After the ceremony, they had a wonderful time with a variety of entertainment, food and dancing. She was quite a character.

Several days later I was making the rounds of the local cemeteries and there I found a marvelous old statue. Here again, I was surprised. It was Lily Irene Jackson's tombstone! One can only wonder at all the twists and turns that happened to get me there. Why? I haven't really figured that out yet, but I still have lots of relatives beyond her time to find. I can't let a puzzle like this go unchallenged. Perhaps she was showing me that we have similar tastes and ideas.

I have yet to find the original date of the wedding. That's scheduled for my next trip home. Eerie isn't it?

If You Could See Your Ancestors

Author unknown

If you could see your ancestors
All standing in a row,
Would you be proud of them
Or don't you really know?
Some strange discoveries are made
In climbing family trees,
And some of them, you know,
Do not particularly please.
If you could see your ancestors
All standing in a row,
There might be some of them, perhaps,
You wouldn't care to know.
But here's another question, which
Requires a different view—
If you could meet your ancestors,
Would they be proud of you?

My Rotten Family Tree

Author unknown
Posted to GenHumor in 1999

I climbed my family tree and found
It wasn't worth the climb,
And so I scrambled down convinced
It wasn't worth the time.

Some branches on my tree I found
Were rotten to the core,
And all the tree was full of sap
And hung with nuts galore.

I used to brag my family up
Before I made the climb
But truth compels me now to tell
Of those not worth a dime.

I beg my friends who boast aloud
Of ancestors so great
To climb their family tree and learn
Of those who weren't so straight.

I've learned what family trees are like
That's why I scrambled down—
They're like a tater vine because
The best are underground!

Put Down Your Drink!

by Bettyanne Bruin
Sandy, Utah

When I researched my father's family line I received a lot of help from the Family History Center, owned by the Church of Jesus Christ of Latter-day Saints.

Even though my parents were not members of the Church, I discovered that in the 1800s my dad's great-grandfather's brother had joined the LDS church, known for its good, clean-cut members. When I told my mother the story of how my dad's family had joined the LDS Church, she called out to my father, "Ray, put down your drink. We might be Mormon!"

CHAPTER ASSIGNMENT:

Look up a chosen surname on a website. Begin to see what work has been done, including any existing Coat of Arms or heritage folktales.

CHAPTER 14

Seasons Of Growth For Trees

How to fertilize and grow the family tree through all seasons of your life

> "I don't know who my grandfather was. I am much more
> concerned to know what his grandson will be."
> —ABRAHAM LINCOLN

It seems genealogy has been stereotyped as a hobby for older people. Someone once said, "It's for people who have one foot in the grave and one out!" Actively researching archives and documents is definitely easier when you don't have to stop to change diapers and nurse a baby every few hours, but no matter what season in life you are in, you CAN do something that helps fertilize and grow your family tree. Projects as simple as organizing photos with young children can be considered "doing genealogy."

You don't have to wait until your hair turns grey to be invited into the "genealogy club!" Read chapter 6 for fun family activities, and chapter 8 for creative craft projects that can involve everyone. If you are one of the senior members on your living family tree, there is much you can do to nurture a budding genealogist to continue your work when you are unable to. Participating in even the simplest of genealogy tasks together sends the message that family history is important and that we are all part of one great whole.

Here are a few ideas on how to include young children in your heritage hunting:

+ Create your own game cards with the names and photos of different ancestors. You can play a matching game or create rules for own new game. Laminate the cards so little fingers don't ruin all of your hard work! Can't you just imagine your family sitting around the table playing "Go Fish" with cards that have a picture of Great Grandpa Calvin wearing his World War I uniform?

+ Encourage young children to keep a "Grandparents Journal" where they draw pictures about what they did, and write reminder notes of things they want to tell you about the next time you are together.

+ Create a "Pillow Talk" book for children who can write. The book can be a small notebook and is kept under the child's pillow. When the child isn't around, write a question or two for her to answer, such as "What would you like to do this weekend?" or "What is your favorite dessert that we could make Monday night?" Before going to bed at night, she will open up the "Pillow Talk" notebook and add her entry. She can answer your questions and then ask you to answer some of her questions. Before long, you will have a fun conversation that makes an excellent journal in disguise!

+ Plan a time each week when you sit down with each child to go over their goals, allowance, chores and calendaring. Create a special binder where you can keep track of progress, using stickers or some other form of reward that will motivate the child. Be sure to provide lots of praise, hugs and kisses. Trina calls it "M n M Time" as an acronym for "Me & Mom" time and as an excuse to eat MnM's while chatting! Tracey calls it "lap chat" in her home. Those charts will be a type of journal and those special visits will be priceless!

+ Create a baby book for each child. Collect pictures, birth certificate, blessing certificate, that amazingly small wrist ID band from the hospital, and other items. Organize them into a personal keepsake for the child. It could be given to the child at any monumental date (wedding day, 21st birthday, birth of their own child, etc.) If their mother has already created one, then simply sitting down with each child and turning the pages of their books with your "oohs and aaahs" delivers the message that they are an important part of the whole family.

+ Write love letters to each child secretly and place them into a book that can be given later as a gift. You could also present the child with a special binder where he can place all the letters you write to him as he receives them in the mail.

+ Keep a journal for your child. Be sure to include basics like Baby's first tooth, smile, trip, birthday, etc. You can also create a calendar journal by placing specially-marked stickers on days that she reached certain milestones.

+ Help your child begin to keep his own journal. Schedule a time every day or week when you can help him "write an entry." For children too young to write, have them dictate their entry for you to write. If they can't think of anything to say, have them answer simple questions such as "What is your favorite color and why?" or "What was your favorite thing that you did today?" and "Why?" Have them draw pictures to illustrate the entry.

- Organize family photos together. Place them chronologically, by people, or by themes. Decorate binders or scrapbooks where photo collections can be kept, using acid-free paper and paper protectors. Be sure to identify who is in each picture, as well as label the outside of the binder. Use all of those second prints to create another photo album that is just for those little fingers to play with.

- Attend family reunions! Be sure to get your name and address on the list of your family organizations. Help organize activities that will keep the little ones occupied while the adults sit and talk. You don't want a boring reunion to leave a sour taste in their mouth for future family gatherings!

- Plan a family reunion if nobody else is doing one! Involve the children in planning all aspects of the event from designing the invitations to organizing games and activities. All of the children in the extended family could be in charge of making placemats for the meal as a gathering activity at the beginning of the festivities. Ask the children what they want to do to contribute, so that they know they are part of the growing legacy of the family. They just might think of the greatest tradition your family has ever had! Read Chapter 10 for more family reunion ideas!

- Learn to cook foods from your native ancestral country. Tell the story about how Grandma Doris always made Hot Cross Buns while the children knead the dough.

- Display photos of your immediate family and then aunts, uncles and cousins. Especially if your extended family lives long distance, visual reminders can help connect the family unit for children.

+ Create a photo family tree on a wall or in an album to help children visualize grandparents.
+ Have a "family history mystery" evening where you choose an ancestor that you give clues about while the family tries to guess who it is. Then show a picture, read sections from a biography or tell stories about that ancestor.
+ Attend cultural events from your family's personal ethnic background. Help children to be proud of their cultural heritage and embrace some of the traditions into their daily lives.
+ Learn or teach your native language if you're not already doing so in the home. Teaching the children even a few phrases they can use will surely impress everyone and, more importantly, give them a sense of pride and confidence.
+ Learn the national folk dance from an ancestral country such as Scottish highland dancing, the Irish jig, etc.
+ Attend a scrapbooking class together and design a few pages that can be put in their special book of remembrance.
+ Create a separate journal for each child where you record all of the cute and funny things he says and does. Children will ask to read their "funny" book, which can provide hours of laughter years later.
+ Create a family newsletter with events and news for the extended family. Add pictures since a picture says a thousand more words. E-mail is even cheaper.
+ Send each other e-mail, even if you live in the same town! Writing letters is great practice for their schoolwork, and it also establishes a great tradition of communication in your family.

- Create a family website where family members can post photos and share news.
- Take annual family photos. It's exhausting to try to get all your little ones dressed neatly and smiling at the same time, but it IS worth it! If little Bo happens to be cranky that day and refuses to smile, so be it! His scowl will be considered adorable in only a few years. Think long term, and don't get stressed out about it!
- In addition to the annual family photo, take an extended family photo. With that many bodies in one picture it's nice to have a specific color theme so everyone matches. Another variation is to blend a color theme. For example, the Duncan family could all wear red t-shirts, the Bates family could wear green, etc.
- Whenever you are doing something together you can take a picture and explain that you're going to include the photo in your special genealogy book. Let them hear the word "genealogy" frequently enough so they soon learn that "family history is just something our family does!"
- Begin that tradition of writing the annual family letter that summarizes the events from your past year and include it with your Christmas cards. Some people think those "form letters" are obnoxious, so just keep the bragging to a minimum and everyone will enjoy being updated! The letters will make an excellent record that future generations will be grateful to have.
- Begin a growth chart. Long ago people drew markings on a designated wall in their home and could enjoy watching their children's growth over the years. Nowadays, young families move frequently, so creating a growth chart on something that can be taken with you from home

to home makes more sense. Some people use a yardstick that can be attached to a wall temporarily, a ribbon, or a fold-up poster. Be sure to include the date when the height was taken.

+ Take pictures of the same event every year, such as the children in their Halloween costumes, their first day of school, standing next to their Easter baskets, etc. Displaying those pictures as a themed group reveals the children's growth in a dramatic way.

Trina had the following experience of following a prompting and helping someone that only she could assist:

Whispers In a Foreign Language

One Friday afternoon I felt a strong impression that I needed to go to the LDS Family History Center on Saturday. I looked at my planner and saw that I would have plenty of time during the next day. Instead of sleeping in, like I love to do on Saturday mornings, my eyes seemed to open early and I felt impressed to wake up and get dressed quickly. I wanted to have a leisurely breakfast, get a few chores done and then mosey on over to do some genealogy work later in the afternoon, but I felt an unexplained urgent need to get to the Family History Center right away, rather than wait until the afternoon.

As I drove to the building I felt my foot pushing harder on the accelerator, not understanding why I felt in such a hurry. As I entered the doors to the building I saw an older woman talking excitedly, surrounded by a group of other women. As I approached I could hear the first woman speaking Spanish and it was soon *obvious that no one could understand her. As they all looked quite frustrated I spontaneously offered my Spanish skills and soon learned that the lady had traveled from Colombia, South America to do research on her grandmother's side of the family.*

She was only going to be in town for the day and available to work on this project today. Normally, the church building had several volunteers who are trained in Spanish, but for some reason none of them were able to come that day and no one was able to help this woman. I ended up spending the day side by side with this sweet Colombian lady as her special escort, translating everything she needed. Her Spanish-speaking ancestors understood the need to be found in any language! A loving Heavenly Father knew she needed help and where she could get it.

We Have Company!

by Ron Bremer
Paradise, Utah

During a break at one of my genealogy seminars in Lebanon, Oregon, a lady came up to me and related the following experience. One night, her husband came running into her bedroom and said, "Honey, get up! We have company!" Her husband had been dead for many years, so this alone, was shock enough! However, she put on her robe and walked with him into the front room, where she beheld over one hundred people, all dressed in white. One of these people stepped forward and said, "We are all ancestors of your departed husband. You are the only person on earth who can do this great work. Will you please help us?" She did!

Trina had a remarkable dream that helped motivate her to move forward with her family history.

Dr. Tom

Like most parents who excitedly anticipate the birth of a baby, my husband and I tossed around name ideas during my second pregnancy. We hoped it would be a son, and my husband was voting for the name Calvin, after his father and grandfather. I was campaigning for other names, however, and as the delivery day grew closer we were still undecided.

One night I dreamed about my husband's grandfather, Calvin Sr. He had died many years before I married my husband, so I only knew him by photographs. He spoke to me and asked me if I would, please, work on his family's history. I was so excited that he had come to me and I wanted my husband, Tom, to hear his grandfather's voice, so in the dream I got a tape-recorder to record our conversation. When I awoke I ran to my tape recorder to see if our visit had actually been recorded. It seemed so real! I was disappointed when I opened the tape recorder and there was no cassette inside, but I had a renewed determination to do Calvin Sr.'s genealogy.

As the end of a pregnancy nears, every woman begins to look forward to the delivery day with a mixture of happiness and fear. My first pregnancy ended in an excruciating, long labor, so my simple prayer was "Please Heavenly Father, let this labor be short!" I've learned to be very careful about what I pray for now… My labor was so short that I didn't even have time to get out of the bedroom at home, and my husband delivered him! You know God had to be laughing about that one! My husband was so calm and took care of everything so well that you would have thought he was a doctor by profession. My family now calls him "Dr. Tom."

Our beautiful baby boy was born early in the morning, while everything in the house was still and quiet. People always ask us if we were frightened during our emergency home delivery, but we were, surprisingly, very calm. We felt a comforting reverence, as a sacred and peaceful spirit filled the room.

I felt the presence of Calvin Sr. watching over us and I knew that everything was going to be ok. I was so grateful to my loving and capable husband, that when he asked me what the baby's name was going to be I told him, "You delivered him, so you can name him anything you want!"

His name is Calvin Ward Boice III !

P.S. This son, Calvin, is the illustrator of this book!

CHAPTER ASSIGNMENT:

Decide what genealogy task you can do this week, no matter what season of life you are in. Write down your goal and plan of action.

_____

_____

_____

_____

_____

_____

_____

_____

_____

_____

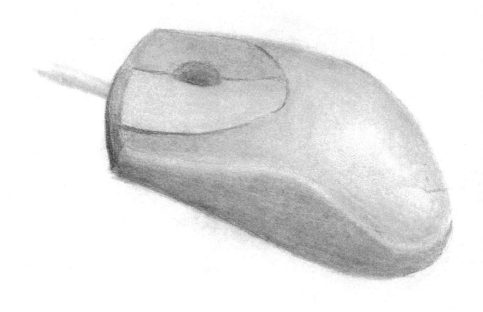

Don't Leaf Work Undone!

Web site resources

Places To Start

www.ancestry.com

Ancestry, Inc. contains several databases. You can search the Social Security Death Index free.

www.byubroadcasting.org/ancestors

A TV mini-series that was produced by Brigham Young University has wonderful instructions for beginners. You can order the series for home use or can borrow it from any LDS Family History Library.

www.familysearch.org

The official website of the LDS Family History Center.

www.cyndislist.com

The largest directory of genealogy links on the Internet!

www.vitalrec.com

Lists addresses and telephone numbers of state and county records offices.

www.genuki.org.uk/gs/

A wonderful site with outlines on how to begin and decide which sources you should be looking for.

www.gendex.com/gendex

Index to family records submitted by individual researchers.

www.genhomepage.com

Collection of miscellaneous information for genealogists.

www.genealogytoolbox.com

Searchable query database, the Journal of Online Genealogy and a list of genealogy links.

http://michigan.gov/hal/0,1607,7-160-17449_18635---,00.html

Various information about genealogy and the library's collection and forms by the Library of Michigan's Genealogy Collection.

http://mel.org/humanities/history/genealogy/genealogy-index. html

Basic genealogy links for the beginner from the Michigan eLibrary (MeL)

www.glorecords.blm.gov

Bureau of Land Management and General Land Office Records list over 2 million land records issued between 1820-1908.

http://www.archives.gov/researchroom/genealogy/index.htm.

Listing of resources and free publications available at the National Archives and how to access and interpret them.

http://genealogy.about.com/library/surnames/bl_meaning.htm

Glossary of meanings of surnames.

http://distantcousin.com

Distant Cousin is a free online archive of genealogy records and scanned images of historical documents from a wide variety of sources, such as newspaper obituaries, city directories, census records, ship lists, school yearbooks, military records, and more. There are more than 6 million genealogy records from over 1,500 sources online.

www.amberskyline.com/treasuremaps/

Free tutorials and genealogy courses. Fun and interesting things such as how to do tombstone rubbings, how to decipher old handwriting, and genealogy DNA.

www.FreeSurnameSearch.com

Access thousands of free genealogy databases and record transcriptions.

www.KnowX.com

Find birth, death, marriage records

www.genealogy.com

Pay for membership for access to databases, message boards, classes, store, library of articles.

http://www.rootsweb.com

Home of the ROOTS-L genealogy list service and the Roots Surname list by the Rootsweb Genealogical Data Cooperative

http://www.usgenweb.com/index.html

USGENWEB is one of the first projects to get genealogical information online for each county of the United States.

http://cpcug.org/user/jlacombe/mark.html

    A barrel of genealogy links!

www.ancestry.com/search/rectype/vital/ssdi/main.htm

    The Social Security Death Index lists individuals whose deaths since 1962 have been reported to the Social Security Administration.

www.heritagequestonline.com/prod/genealogy/books

    Subscription service but lists over 25,000 family histories.

www.home.earthlink.net/~howardorjeff/instruct.htm

    This site offers great tips for beginning your search with a research kit. Special sections for children and teens.

Genealogy Societies

www.helplist.org

    A group of volunteers willing to look up documents in their particular region. These people get tickets straight to heaven.

http://fgs.org

    Homepage of the national organization, Federation of Genealogical Societies.

http://www.ngsgenealogy.org

    National Genealogical Society. See how to submit research requests and info about the organization.

http://www.nehgs.org

    The homepage of one of the nation's largest genealogical organizations, the New England Historic Genealogical Society (NEHGS)

Cemetery Records

www.findagrave.com

> Lists addresses, maps, GPS coordinates for over 150,000 cemeteries in the USA. There are also some online records.

www.interment.net

> Includes a database of 3 million cemetery records from 6,700 cemeteries.

www.cemeteryjunction.com

> Lists over 38,000 U.S. cemeteries. Includes cemetery addresses and links to records online.

http://www.teafor2.com

> 108,332 cemetery pictures for free.

Census Records

www.census-online.com

> Lists free websites, commercial websites, CD's, and books for census records, images, as well as links to many other census websites. Resources are arranged by state and county.

www.heritagequest.com

> You can purchase CDs that contain many images and indexes of censuses, including many that were previously un-indexed in 1910. You can also use many of these CD's for free at the LDS Family History Centers in your area.

www.us-census.org/search.html

> The most comprehensive free set of census transcriptions on the Internet! You can search by name, state, and year.

Immigration

http://www.ellisisland.org

> Operated by The American Family Immigration History Center, you can search for ancestors who arrived in New York Harbor from 1892 to 1924.

www.genealogy.com

> Look for the Passenger and Immigration Lists Index, 2001 ed., (FHL CD #354). It is the largest index of published U.S. passenger lists. You can also look for Family Tree Maker's immigration CD's at this site, which includes various ports and ethnicities.

Maps

www.testbed.alexandria.ucsb.edu/gazclient/index.jsp

> The Alexandria Library Gazeteer contains over 4 million locations worldwide.

www.mapquest.com

> Search for present-day street maps, including directions.

http://lcweb2.loc.gov/ammem/gmdhtml/gmdhome.html

> Library of Congress collection of maps from 1500 to 2002.

www.topozone.com

> Do searches in terms of topography (mountains, rivers, regions) rather than state borders that might not have existed during your ancestor's time period.

www.davidrumsey.com

> Cartographic Associates includes 8,000 rare U.S. maps that are organized by state.

Directories (for living people!)

www.infospace.com

> Residential and business directories listed by name, category or location. Maps and directions are included.

www.switchboard.com

> Residential and business directories listed by name, category or location. Maps and directions are included.

www.yellowpages.com

> Business and residential listings.

www.infospace.com

> Business and residential listings.

www.anywho.com

> Includes international listings and maps, in addition to phone numbers for people and businesses.

CHAPTER ASSIGNMENT:

Look up one of the websites and begin to explore the contents and resources available. Look up www.familysearch.org and research one chosen ancestor to see what the process is. Get ready to be amazed at the wonderful finds!

$$\overline{\text{C H A P T E R \quad 1 6}}$$

Barking Up The RIGHT Tree
Doggone genealogy

Everyone knows a dog is man's best friend. We found another reason to champion the cause of canines...they do genealogy! Well, sort of. People sent us so many stories about dogs that inspired their family history research that we thought you would get a kick out this chapter! Dogs are loyal and dependable to their master and faithful to their family...no matter what side of the veil they're on. Dogs are known to chase cats up a tree, but the things dogs can chase from a family tree are even more remarkable!

It made no doggone sense

by Becky Carden
Anniston, Alabama
I have an ancestor by the name of Lovick Pierce Jordan, who is buried by the Bethel Baptist church, in this tiny little place called Welch, Alabama. My family and I had gone to the cemetery several

times and found some members of the Jordan family, but never Lovick, nor his wife.

My dad and I were standing at this one particular Jordan family grave-site, where he was trying to fix a broken piece of the grave marker, when I saw something in the distance. It was a large, beautiful, white dog. He walked right up to me! I love dogs, but am a little leery of strays. As I "talked" to him, he seemed very sweet and gentle. I proceeded to go over to my great great grandparents' graves and the dog followed right along beside me, every step of the way. After leaving their graves, I decided to give up on finding Lovick, but the dog stayed with me, leading me to where my dad was. All of a sudden, my dad said he had found some more markers with the Jordan family name. I went over to see who he had found, and lo and behold, there was my Lovick P. Jordan, his wife, Melissa Ann Freeman Jordan, and also their daughter!

When I finished taking pictures and started to walk back to the car I realized the white dog was gone! I looked everywhere for him, but it was like he vanished into thin air! My mother had been waiting in the car and said she had never seen him. We decided to go back to the cemetery the next week, but the dog was still nowhere to be found. I've gone back several times since then, and have never seen this beautiful, white dog again.

I know this may sound ridiculous, but I feel the white dog fulfilled his mission, as he was sent to help me find my Lovick Pierce Jordan.

Angels with Four Legs

by Tina Mathis
Canton, Ohio

My wonderful husband and I took a trip to Calhoun County in West Virginia, looking for my paternal grandmother's family cemetery near the town that used to be called Freed. That was also the maiden name of my grandmother, as well as the name of the cemetery we were looking for. It was located in the backwoods, up the hills, and across a creek. As I waded through the creek my husband tried to find the shallow stepping stone path. Suddenly, we noticed that we had a companion: a very large, beautiful, long-haired, red dog that I referred to as "Sam" the rest of the day.

It took several attempts at hill climbing to figure out which cemetery was the correct one. My husband was exhausted and sat down to rest, but not Sam the dog. He stayed right with me. Finally, we stumbled onto the right mountain. My husband found a shade tree that he and Sam lounged under for a bit, but not for long, as some ants had other ideas. My husband and Sam politely left that tree to find better accommodations. As for me, I marched on, armed with my camera and notebook.

I started searching for a female ancestor who was key in proving a certain fact that had baffled me since I started this particular genealogy quest. I started talking to her (I'm not the only one who does that, am I?) "Mary, where are you?" I repeated her name over and over. As my hopes were leaving me I sat down in despair. My husband laughed and said I was probably sitting on her. "I hope so because I can't seem to find her anywhere" I sighed. He then started to pat the area around him. You can guess the rest of the story! There was a corner poking out of the ground, a small broken headstone containing only a name and age. It was exactly what I had been looking for! Sam left us soon after that. I guess his job was done. We found what we came for.

We were both amused by the "coincidence." I would like to believe that my ancestor knew we were there and wanted to be remembered by someone. It sounds odd and I would be skeptical if I had not been there to see the day unfold the way it did.

Man's Best Friend

by Mary Hall and Sandra Brown
Riverdale, Georgia

My sister decided to raise and breed Shiatsu puppies, but needed more space for them. She started looking for some land out in the country. She found a place in Williamson, Georgia and bought it in October in the late 1990s. In November of the same year, I started posting messages to a genealogical forum on the Internet and had received a lot of answers from seven 2nd and 3rd cousins whom we had never met. In our correspondence they told us that our third great grandfather had land in Pike County, Georgia in the early 1800s and was buried on the "Old Horton Home" property, wherever that was.

When my sister went to the courthouse and started researching deeds for her newly acquired land, she discovered she had bought a part of the old Horton Home property! On the next road behind her house in the woods there is a family burial plot, allegedly belonging to our own family. Who would have guessed those Shiatzu puppies would have helped us find our own ancestral home!

Blue Lacey

by Marlo Riley
San Antonio, Texas

In April of 1998, I started researching the Blue Lacy dog breed, or as old records state, the "Lacy hog dog." My Australian Shepard had just been put to sleep. With the loss of my blood-trailing dog, the quest for a replacement began. Wanting to start with a breed that would be bred for the purpose to track wounded game, I started inquiring about different dog breeds. While looking at some kennels for a new pup at Home Depot, one of the employees and I started talking. During the conversation I expressed to him the type of abilities I needed in a dog. The man replied, "You need a Blue Lacy." Never having heard of this breed, my interest was piqued. He told me that they were the best blood-trailing dogs in Texas. The next day I looked everywhere and could not find any information on this breed.

About a week later I came across an ad in the paper for Blue Lacy pups for sale. The breeder lived in Boerne, Texas. He bred his Lacy female for some government trapper friends that needed Lacy's for their work. After the trappers picked the pups they wanted, he sold the rest. By the time I called, he already had all of the pups sold. He did invite me up to see his dogs. Finally, a chance to see this mysterious breed!

After arriving, I learned that this breeder was Mr. Robert Cravey. He and my father, Wayne Cavin, had gone through the Fire Fighter Academy together and had worked in the same Fire Department for at least 20 years! We recognized each other immediately. What a small world! We talked for a moment and then this beautiful gray dog walked up to me. It was his Blue Lacy female. I fell in love.

Now, I was sure that this was the perfect breed for me. Medium sized, short hair, with a lot of hunt to them. Mr. Cravey had been given an article from a friend about Blue Lacy's and shared a copy with me. The article spoke about all the qualities and background of this breed. It stated how they were an all-around working dog. This dog would be great for blood-trailing and could meet my other hunting task and working needs. The search for a pup went into overdrive.

Several weeks went by and my search was leading nowhere. One of my family members, Winifred Roque, just happened to call. "How are you doing?" she asked. Frustrated that my Internet search for puppies had come up blank, I responded, "Not good!" Winifred seemed concerned. Not to alarm her, I quickly replied, "Sorry, I am just upset. I fell in love with this rare dog breed and I can't seem to find any pups or information." She had to ask, "What kind of dog are you looking for?" "A Blue Lacy," I answered. "You're kidding!" she said. "No, why? You know what a Blue Lacy is?" Winifred started to tell me all about the Blue Lacy dogs and how the "Lacy Brothers," George Washington, Frank Marion, Ewin Young, and John Hiram (Harry) Lacy, developed the breed soon after arriving in Burnet County, Texas in 1858. Then she said, "Your great great grandfather is Frank Marion Lacy, one of the four brothers! You didn't know?" I about fell on the floor!

She had family photos, lineage, and the background of the family and their dogs. She had received this information from some of my aunts and uncles that researched our family tree. They had all driven up to Marble Falls and met with Helen Gibbs and R.L. Mezger. Both Mrs. Gibbs and Mr. Mezger were grandchildren of George Washing Lacy. Helen Gibbs provided most of the Lacy *family history for the records that are held at the Burnet County Library. Come to find out, R.L Mezger inherited what is left of the Lacy family ranch and still lives there. Helen and R.L. both remember the Lacy dogs their fathers and grandfathers owned.*

All of my family knew my love for dogs, training animals and hunting. Yet, none of my family ever told me this incredible history! They had talked about the marble granite that was used to build the state capital building and that our family was involved in the donation, but never anything about dogs. Never did anyone tell me these same men developed an all-around working dog breed. Needless to say, I got with Winifred right away and copied all the information she had. Now, my real journey began! I wasn't just looking for a great dog now, but my family heritage as well!

Through the information and background Winifred had, I found H.C. Wilkes. H.C. Wilkes still lived on part of the old Lacy ranch. His father-in-law had been the ranch foreman for the Lacy family. Mrs. Wilkes inherited 122 acres of the Lacy ranch near Marble Falls, Texas, which had been given to her father for his hard work. H.C. Wilkes was also in the "Hall of Fame" in Quinlan, Texas, for the work he had done regarding the Blue Lacy breed.

My family and I drove up for a visit with Mr. and Mrs. Wilkes. I could not wait to meet them, plus have the chance to see some of my forefather's land! Mr. Wilkes thought it was so neat I chose this breed, before I even knew my family history. He said, "Every Lacy family member should own a Lacy dog." They had a beautiful tri-colored Lacy female he sent home with me that day. Mr. Wilkes had registered his dogs with Larry Boyd, but lost his paperwork and didn't remember a name or how to contact him. Through further research and calls, I found a man by the name of Jimmy

Brooks. Mr. Brooks is a government trapper who had owned Blue Lacy's for thirty years. He knew Raymond Trimble and Larry Boyd well, and had heard about the registry. Both Mr. Trimble and Mr. Boyd were government trappers as well. Mr. Brooks gave me Larry Boyd's number. I wanted to talk with Mr. Boyd to find out if I could register the female I had received form H.C. Wilkes.

Mr. Boyd had retired from the Wildlife Services and bought a nice antique shop in Boerne, Texas. We met for lunch that October day in 1998. I shared with Mr. Boyd how hard it was to get my first Lacy pup. He expressed to me his love and background with this wonderful breed. Knowing how hard it had become to find a pure breed Lacy, he asked me to start up the registry again. This was yet another shock! I just wanted to find a paper trail on my new pup, and now I had all the paper work. Feeling very honored, I vowed to Larry Boyd that I would not let the breed down.

Through research, many phone calls, and visits with all the original breeders who were still alive, I was able to regain the five years of history that were lost. The rugged virtues and abilities the Lacy Brothers bred this true Texas breed to be are still evident today because of the passion of these individuals: Jack Franks, Raymond Trimble, Larry Boyd, Mr. and Mrs. Wilkes, Steve Kimbrell, Jimmy Brooks, Tom Graham, Kermit Sultemier, Oliver Rode, Gary and Bryan Larremore, and Cowboy Williams. These quality breeders and Lacy enthusiasts are largely responsible for the growth of the Lacy Game Dog Registry.

In 2004 we had over five times the number of proven purebred Blue Lacy's on record since 1999. On March 8, 2001, the Senate of the State of Texas honored the Blue Lacy breed, along with the Lacy Brothers, with Senate Resolution No. 436. Within this resolution it states: "*The Blue Lacy breed is believed to be the first dog breed to have originated in Texas and has a capacity for hard work that typifies the rugged virtues of a Texas ranch-hand. We will keep moving forward in honoring these historic Texas pioneers by maintaining the standards the Lacy brothers intended for their Blue Lacy dogs.*"

The first Blue Lacy registered with the Lacy Game Dog Registry was recorded on May 20, 1985. Jack Franks, the originator of the registry, inspected and registered all the Blue Lacy dogs that where registered from May 20, 1985 until March 26, 1986. The registry has changed hands several times. By 1987 the registry was sold to Raymond Trimble. Mr. Trimble is credited for all recorded registries from February 11, 1987 thru April 13, 1990, at which time he then handed over the registry to Larry Boyd. Shortly after Mr. Boyd accepted the responsibility for the registry, he contracted Lyme disease. Due to his illness he wasn't able to meet the demands of the registry. He inspected and registered his last Blue Lacy, July 19, 1993. Over five years passed without any new records or lineages filed for the Blue Lacy breed. This all changed October of 1998, when Larry Boyd passed the torch to Marlo Riley. January 1, 1999 the Lacy Game Dog Registry was officially re-born.

For more information please visit the websites www.lacydog.com and www.bluelacydogs.org.

CHAPTER ASSIGNMENT:

Many people associate dogs with pedigrees and now here's your chance to keep up with man's best friend. Complete your pedigree chart as far as you can go. The blank spaces will show you where more research is needed!

CHAPTER 17

Grafting Branches Into The Family Tree

Adopting new family members

Have you ever watched the process of grafting a new branch into a tree? It requires great care and skill, resulting in a stronger and even more beautiful tree. Dave Thomas, the founder of Wendy's restaurants, was adopted as a child. He said "Every child deserves a home and love. Period." Jamie Lee Curtis, actress, is an adoptive mother who said "We look at adoption as a very sacred exchange. It was not done lightly on either side." Nicole Kidman, another celebrity adoptive parent, said "Somehow destiny comes into play. These children end up with you and you end up with them. It's something quite magical."

Climbing family trees is difficult enough, but when your family tree grafts in twigs or branches by adopting new family members it can get a bit tricky. Searching for birth records of open and closed adoptions can also be quite controversial. A birth is simultaneously an intimate occasion and a public event. Governments have long kept records of when, where, and by whom babies are born; however, the right to view those records in the case of adoption continues to be hotly debated.

Many people who are adopted are torn between researching their blood line (if they can determine it), or researching the family line of their adopted family. It is a very personal decision.

Another adoptive parent, Joan McNamara, explained, "It has been said that adoption is more like a marriage than a birth: two (or more) individuals, each with their own unique mix of needs, patterns, and genetic history, coming together with love, hope and commitment for a joint future. You become a family, not because you share the same genes, but because you share love for each other."

Often adopted children feel very alone and that they aren't connected in a "real" way. It's hard to face the world when you don't know where your face came from! The following stories are to help encourage and comfort those who feel they are sitting on a lone branch of a foreign tree. Their new place as a grafted branch adds much depth to their tree and is a great blessing to the family.

A few of the helpful resources on the Internet for locating birth records of adult adoptees are:

www.birthfamily.com/registry
www.cyndislist.com/adoption.htm
http://adoptees-contact-line.com
www.adoption.com
www.adopting.com
www.adoption.org
www.abcadoptions.com
http://freepages.genealogy.rootsweb.com/~orphanshome/ (Orphans' Home Website)

www.genealogicaljourneys.com/mbfr.htm
(Bulletin board postings)
www.ukbirth-adoptionregister.com/ (England)
www.vs.gov.bc.ca/genealogy/adopt.html (British Columbia)

Karen Halvorsen Schreck has written a great book entitled *Lucy's Family Tree* (Tilbury House Publishing, 2001) that tenderly addresses the special needs and desires of adopted children to understand where they belong and how they fit into this world. Here are a few of her terrific ideas for ways to incorporate all the extended families into an adoptive family tree.

One option for the adopted child is to depict the birth family and the adopted family on a wheel. Two half wheels, one for the birth family, and one for the adoptive family, put together, makes a complete circle with the child in the center!

Using houses instead of trees to show linkages between family members, not only makes genetic lines easier to understand, but also illustrates that other family members, such as parents, have left one home to start another to make links between members with new members.

Another option for the adopted child is to depict both the birth family and the adoptive family on a tree. The birth parents are the roots of the child's tree, providing the origins of the child's life. The leaves and branches give the child the fullness of his life.

Patty's Peace

by Judith Hudson
Palestine, Illinois
(Daughter of Patricia Alice 'Colbert' Lucas)

For several years Patricia Alice Colbert felt as if she didn't exist. At the age of seventeen she discovered she wasn't who she thought she was. And the people she called Mom and Dad weren't the people she thought they were.

In 1945, during her senior year of high school, she had decided to apply for a Civil Service position, which required a birth certificate. She made her trip to town in Bloomington, Indiana to get the copy she needed. She was told that there was no birth record for a Patricia Alice Colbert. In fact, there wasn't anything about Patricia Alice Colbert or a Colbert child that could be found in her age bracket! Puzzled and bewildered, Patty went to her mom with questions. What she heard changed her life forever. She was told she was not their natural child and they had changed her name when they took her into their home. She had been told all she "needed" to know and it was never to be brought up for discussion again.

It wasn't until years later that my mom finally learned her given birth name: Laura Alice Chandler. Her mother had died when she was a baby and her father could not care for her. He handed her over to the adoptive parents to raise. Patty said "The abruptness of the way they told me hurt more than the truth." That same year she petitioned the Monroe County, Indiana Courts for a legal name change. In March 1946 she legally became Patricia Alice Colbert, the only name she ever knew.

In 1947 Patty married and had four children. Still, something *was missing in her life. She didn't feel complete. But she did have several names: her father's given name and her mother's given and maiden name. Around 1970 she began her search for the family she never knew.*

Patty had been researching the Chandler family for several years when she was asked to speak at a genealogy seminar at the Church of Jesus Christ of Latter-day Saints in Bloomington. After she had spoken a young woman introduced herself as Linda. She too, was researching the Chandlers!

As Patty and Linda talked, something between them connected. The friendship that developed was more like a kindred spirit. They researched together. Their families broke bread together. It was a blending of two families becoming one. In Patty's heart Linda had become her second daughter. Each was researching their own book when they decided to combine them into one. They would share expenses and cut costs. Because Patty had done the majority of research it was decided she would be listed as Author and Linda as the Co-author. Work progressed smoothly and a lot of support from family members was given. In about two more months it would be ready for the printer.

In April 1989, Patty became ill and only one month later she passed away. Only the indexing of their book had been left to do, but now Patty's manuscript lay quietly on her desk. There was no hand to lovingly caress its pages. Several months after Patty's death, I was contacted by Linda. She said she and my mom had made a promise to each other that no matter what happened their book would be published and the Chandler family story would be shared. Linda then left the house with Mom's book.

For ten years we heard nothing from Linda. I had long given up hope of finding her or Patty's manuscript. One evening I received a phone call from Linda. She had called to tell me that Patty's book was going to the printer the next morning and that it would be ready in about six weeks. Five weeks later I was reading my copy of:

The William and Sally Chandler Family History
of Salt Creek Township, Monroe County, Indiana
By: Patricia Alice Lucas

What Ever Happened to Little Tommy?

by Sharon L. Holt

Member of Chemeketa Chapter NSDAR, Salem, Oregon

Ever since I was old enough to remember, I heard my parents ask the question, "I wonder what ever happened to little Tommy?" "Little Tommy" was the son from my aunt's second marriage. My aunt passed away in 1938 in Yakima, Washington, leaving behind her second husband and the two half-siblings. The oldest son was taken in by my parents and raised in our home until he was military age. "Little Tommy" on the other hand, literally disappeared from the lives of our family for sixty-five years!

What happened to Tommy? His father kept him and together they disappeared. Several attempts were made by family members to locate the child, but attempts were futile. About 15 years ago, my sister, Carol, sent for our deceased aunt's death certificate in Washington, but there was no certificate on file. Letters were sent out to every known family by the last name of Worsley in the state of Washington. Again, we hit a brick wall. Just over two years ago, the attempts to locate "little Tommy" hit an urgent note for my sister because he would have been 68 or 69 years old by then and our chances of finding him would become slimmer with his advancing age. We certainly wanted to find him while there was any chance he could still be living. His half-brother had been dead for several years.

Carol and I were able to obtain my aunt's marriage certificate and Tommy's birth certificate, which yielded two clues that helped our search. One clue was that the certificate stated his father was born in Montana and the other gave Tommy's complete name as Thomas Warner Worsley.

We traveled to Yakima, Washington where our aunt had died and we visited the Yakima Valley Genealogical Society. We expected to spend several days doing research. Within five minutes we had a copy of her obituary in our hands. That led us to the mortuary that handled her funeral service and directed us to the city cemetery and plot location. We then visited her final resting place with the whisper of hope we would find her son, Tommy.

Back home, we utilized a well known people-finder search engine on the Internet by typing in Tommy's full name and focusing on the state of Montana. I found a reliable hit. It was with much anxiety when I took a phone in my hand and made that call to Montana. Now, I'm so thankful that I did because that one call ended the long, difficult search. "Little Tommy" answered the phone! He was just as eager to hear from living family members as we were to hear from and about him. Several years earlier, he had hired a private investigator and tried to locate any living relatives but his search had failed. It seems an amateur genealogist is more effective than a professional private investigator!

For some reason, Tommy's father had destroyed all the family records and pictures and told Tommy that he had no known living relatives. He was a migrant worker and would leave Tommy in boarding homes for lengthy periods of time so he could go from place to place, wherever work could be found. Finally, when Tommy was about 16 years old, he wanted to go into the U. S. Navy and so his father had to produce Tommy's birth certificate. It revealed that Tommy was not the person he thought he was. He had a totally different name!

For some reason he had named him Tommy Hill, son of Chester Hill, instead of Thomas Warner Worsley, son of Carl Worsley. Why the father opted for an alias is a mystery he took to his grave. It is extremely upsetting to Tommy and all family members now, to realize Tommy could have had a loving and stable home, instead of just being a child who was pawned off from one boarding home to another.

Several months later, our grown up little Tom, wanted to meet us and drove to Washington to visit his mother's grave for the first time and to meet us. Our visit was bittersweet in that it took over 65 years to locate Tom and he could have been part of a large and loving family. We are so thankful now that we have each other and can look forward to good times at future gatherings.

My advice to people who are trying to locate lost loved ones is never give up the search! Sometimes the outcome is not what we desire, but then cases like ours give hope. My family will forever treasure the fact that we located Tom. He and his family are precious additions to our family and his story has impacted our hearts with love and gratitude for our lost "little Tommy."

Surfin for Murfin

by Ed Murfin
Jacksonville, Florida

I am doing a one-name study for the surname Murfin, researching in England, Germany, Canada, U.S., Australia, New Zealand, and South Africa. I have thousands of names in about 55 separate Murfin family files in my computer right now. That number goes up and down regularly, as I connect grandfather's brothers, sisters and cousins across the world. I'm constantly finding cousins for people who didn't know they had any and some have been proven to be my own relatives. I have identified two main families, one of which is mine which came over from England. My goal is to eventually find common roots for these other Murfin families. I constantly research what records I can get, on a meager budget, in England and often come up with complete family lines. This helps tremendously in linking these families together.

My most interesting story in this part of my genealogical life is this: In about the year 2002, there was a 21-year-old lady living in the Washington, D.C. area who had known all her life she was adopted. She knew that when she turned 21 her adoptive parents would share her birth information with her. They told her at the time of her birth, her surname was Murfin. She was born out of wedlock on a certain date in Indiana or Illinois. That's all the information they knew to give her.

She went on the Internet to see what she could find with her limited, but newfound information and her basic computer skills. Right off, she found that I was doing Murfin research and contacted me to see if I knew anything about her birth family. I happened to be away from home at the time she phoned. My wife talked in detail with this excited young woman and took notes for me. When I came back from being out of town, I studied the story.

I went into my FamilyTreeMaker files of all the Murfin families. I quickly determined that she was not within my personal family, but I did locate some Murfin families in the area mentioned, with whom I had some contact. One lady told me that she had a male cousin who had given up a child in adoption at about that period of time, but had later married the mother of the child. She would see if there could be any connection. Within three days and with those leads, I found the young lady's birth parents!

I learned that they had subsequently gotten married and had at least two other children. They were still living in the same area. I made contact with the parents, and then with the young lady in D.C. You can imagine that she was tremendously excited to find out this kind of information. She was even more excited that the family was anxious to meet her and to know her. A couple of months later she enjoyed Thanksgiving Day dinner with her new family. This one story makes all the work I do worth it!

CHAPTER ASSIGNMENT:

Begin to write a biography on one of your parents, whether they are biological, adopted or a step-parent. Write major events in chronological order for a time-line and begin to fill in the events with stories or answers to questions for interviewing.

CHAPTER 18

Branching Out

Book resources for climbing family trees

There are some excellent genealogy books that can provide you with helpful resources and tools for your research. You should be able to check most of them out of your local library, but you can also find them at your local LDS Family History Center, used book stores, and even on E-bay! You can also purchase CDs now that contain all kinds of data and records at very reasonable prices.

Another book that you should have on hand is your own journal! If you don't already have one, keep a genealogy journal, where you can record your own cool genealogy experiences, feelings about finding your ancestors and promptings you might receive while hunting for family. Such a journal will become priceless to generations yet unborn. What a tremendous gift that would be to pass on to your own descendents!

A Genealogist's Guide to Discovering Your Immigrant and Ethnic Ancestors, by Sharon DeBartolo Carmack. Cincinnati, Ohio: Betterway Books, 1998.

American Genealogical Research at the DAR, Washington, D.C., by Eric G. Grundset and Stephen B. Rhodes. Washington, D.C.: DAR, 1997.

American Naturalization Records, 1790-1990:What They Are and How to Use Them, by John J. Newman. Heritage Quest, 1998.

American Passenger Arrival Records, A Guide to the Records of Immigrants Arriving at American Ports by Sail or Steam, by Michael Tepper. Baltimore, Md.: Genealogical Publishing Company, Inc., 1993.

Ancestry's Red Book: American State, County and Town Sources, rev.ed., by Alice Eichholz. Salt Lake City, Utah: Ancestry, Inc. 1992.

Compendium of Historical Sources, 9th ed., by Ronald A. Bremer. Paradise, Utah: Ron Bremmer Publishing. 1998.

The American Census Handbook, by Thomas Jay Kemp. Wilminton, Del.: Scholarly Resources, 2001.

The Basic Researcher's Gide to Homesteads and Other Federal Land Records, by James C. Barsi. Colroado Springs, Colo.: Nuthatch Grove Press, 1994.

Cemeteries of the U.S. : A Guide to Contact Information for U.S. Cemeteries and Their Records, by Deborah M. Burek, ed. Detroit, Mich.: Gale Research, Inc. 1994.

The Census Book: A Genealogist's Guide to Federal Census Facts, Schedules, and Indexes, by William dollarhide. Gountiful, Utah: Heritage Quest, Inc., 2000.

County Courthouse Book, 3d ed., by Elizabeth Petty Bentley. Baltimore, Md.: Genealogical Publishing Col, Inc., 1995.

The Complete Beginniner's Guide to Genealogy, the Internet, and Your Genealogy Computer Program, by Karen Clifford. Baltrimore, Md.: Genealogical Publishing Co., Inc. 2001.

The Complete Idiot's Guide to Online Genealogy, by Rhonda R. McClure. Indianapolis, Ind.: alpha Books, 2000.

The Complete Idiot's Guide to Writing Your Family History, by Lynda Rutledge Stephenson. Indianapolis, Ind.: Alpha Books, 2000.

Cyndi's List: A Comprehensive List of Over 40,000 Genealogical Sites on the Internet, by Cyndi Howells. 2 vols. Baltimore, Md.: Genealogical Publishing Co., Inc., 2001.

Family Tales, Family Wisdom, by Robert U. Akeret, Ed.D. Paperback. New York: Henry Holt and Co., 1991.

Genealogy Online for Dummies, 4th ed., by Matthew L. Helm and April Leigh Helm.

The Genealogy Sourcebook, by Sharon DeBartolo Carmack. Los Angeles, California: Lowell House, 1997.

The Genealogist's Question and Answer Book, by Marcia Yannizze Melnyk. Cincinnati, Ohio: Betterway Books. 2002.

The Handy Book for Genealogists, 9th ed., by George B. Everton. Logan, Utah: Everton Publishers, 1999.

How to Find Almost Anyone, Anywhere, by Norma Mott Tillman. Nashville, Tenn.: Rutledge Hill Press, 1998.

How to Locate Anyone Who Is or Has Been in the Military, 4th ed., by Richard S. Johnson and Debra Johnson Knox. Military Information Enterprises, 1999.

International Vital Records Handbook, 4th ed., by Thomas Jay Kemp. Baltimore, Md.: Genealogical Publishing Co., Inc., 2000.

Keeping Family Secrets Alive, 2d ed., by Vera Rosenbluth. Port Robers, Wash.: Hartley & Marks Pub., 1997.

Land and Property Research in the Untied States, by E. wade Hone. Salt Lake City, Utah: Everton Publishing Co., Inc. 1999.

The Library of Congress: A Guide to Genealogical and Historical Research, by James C. Neagles. Salt Lake City, Utah: Ancestry, Inc., 1996.

Locating Lost Family Members and Friends, by Katheleen W. Hinckley. Cincinnati, Ohio: Betterway Books. 2000.

Long-Distance Genealogy, by Christine Crawford-Oppenheimer. Cincinnati, Ohio: Betterway Books, 2000.

Once Upon a Memory, by Jean Alessi and Jan Miller. White Hall, Va.: Betterway Publications, 1987.

Preserving Your Family Photographs, by Maureen A. Taylor. Cincinnati, Ohio: Betterway Books, 2001.

The Researcher's Guide to American Genealogy, 3d ed., by Val D. Greenwood. Baltimore, Md.: Genealogical Publishing Co., Inc., 2000.

The Sleuth Book for Genealogists: Strategies for More Successful Family History Research, by Emily Anne Croom. Cincinnati, Ohio: Betterway Books, 2000.

The Source: A Guidebook of American Genealogy, rev. ed., edited by Loretto Dennis Szucs and Sandra Hargreaves Luebking. Salt Lake City, Utah: Ancestry, Inc. 1997.

The Tape-Recorded Interview, by Edward D. Ives. Knoxville: University of Tennessee Press, 1995.

They Became Americans: A Guide to Finding Your Immigrant Ancestor's Arrival Record, by John P. Colletta, Ph.D., Salt Lake City, Utah: Ancestry, Inc., 1993.

Uncovering Your Ancestry Through Family Photographs, by Maureen A. Taylor. Cincinnati, Ohio: Betterway Books, 2000.

U.S. Military Records, by James C. Neagles. Salt Lake City, Utah: Ancestry, Inc., 1994.

Where to Write for Vital Records: Births, Deaths, Marriages, and Divorces, by National Center for Health Statistics. Washing, D.C.: NCHS, updated regularly.

Your Guide to Cemetery Research, by Sharon DeBartolo Carmack. Cincinnati, Ohio: Betterway Books, 2002.

CHAPTER ASSIGNMENT:

Begin keeping a genealogy journal. Write your first entry today!

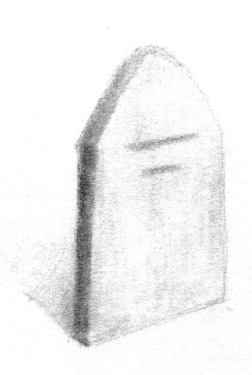

The End Of The Stick

Interesting Epitaphs

Dear Ancestor

Author Unknown

Your tombstone stands among the rest;
neglected and alone
The name and date are chiseled out
on polished, marbled stone
It reaches out to all who care
It is too late to mourn
You did not know that I exist
You died and I was born.
Yet each of us are cells of you
in flesh, in blood, in bone.
Our blood contracts and beats a pulse
entirely not our own.

Dear Ancestor, the place you filled
one hundred years ago
Spreads out among the ones you left
who would have loved you so.
I wonder if you lived and loved,
I wonder if you knew
That someday I would find this spot,
and come to visit you.

Benjamin Franklin wrote his own epitaph.
(Christ Church Burial Grounds; Philadelphia, Pennsylvania)
THE BODY OF
B. FRANKLIN, PRINTER
LIKE THE COVER OF AN OLD BOOK
ITS CONTENTS TURN OUT
AND STRIPT OF ITS LETTERING & GUILDING
LIES HERE. FOOD FOR WORMS
FOR, IT WILL AS HE BELIEVED
APPEAR ONCE MORE
IN A NEW AND MORE ELEGANT EDITION
CORRECTED AND IMPROVED

Lester Moore was a Wells Fargo Co. station agent, and is buried at Boot
Hill Cemetery in Tombstone, Arizona.
HERE LIES LESTER MOORE
FOUR SLUGS FROM A .44
NO LES NO MORE.

⭐

In a London, England cemetery:
HERE LIES ANN MANN,
WHO LIVED AN OLD MAID
BUT DIED AN OLD MANN.
DEC. 8, 1767

"THAT'S ALL FOLKS!"
THE MAN OF A THOUSAND VOICES
MEL BLANC
(Hollywood Memorial Park; Hollywood, California)

In a Ribbesford, England, cemetery:
ANNA WALLACE
THE CHILDREN OF ISRAEL WANTED BREAD
AND THE LORD SENT THEM MANNA,
OLD CLERK WALLACE WANTED A WIFE,
AND THE DEVIL SENT HIM ANNA.

Playing with names in a Ruidoso, New Mexico, cemetery:
HERE LIES
JOHNNY YEAST
PARDON ME
FOR NOT RISING.

Memory of an accident in a Uniontown, Pennsylvania cemetery:
HERE LIES THE BODY
OF JONATHAN BLAKE
STEPPED ON THE GAS
INSTEAD OF THE BRAKE.

In a Silver City, Nevada, cemetery:
HERE LAYS BUTCH,
WE PLANTED HIM RAW.
HE WAS QUICK ON THE TRIGGER,
BUT SLOW ON THE DRAW.

GONE ARE THE LIVING, BUT THE DEAD REMAIN,
AND NOT NEGLECTED; FOR A HAND UNSEEN,
SCATTERING ITS BOUNTY LIKE A SUMMER RAIN,
STILL KEEPS THEIR GRAVES
AND THEIR REMEMBRANCE GREEN.

HENRY WADSWORTH LONGFELLOW
(Mount Auburn Cemetery, Cambridge, Middlesex County,
Massachusetts, USA)

A widow wrote this epitaph in a Vermont cemetery:
SACRED TO THE MEMORY OF MY HUSBAND JOHN BARNES
WHO DIED JANUARY 3, 1803
HIS COMELY YOUNG WIDOW, AGED 23,
HAS MANY QUALIFICATIONS OF A GOOD WIFE,
AND YEARNS TO BE COMFORTED.

A lawyer's epitaph in England:
SIR JOHN STRANGE

HERE LIES AN HONEST LAWYER,
AND THAT IS STRANGE.

NATURE AND NATURE'S LAWS LAY HID IN NIGHT:
GOD SAID, 'LET NEWTON BE!' AND ALL WAS LIGHT.
WRITTEN BY ALEXANDER POPE
SIR ISAAC NEWTON
(Westminster Abbey, London, England)

Someone determined to be anonymous in Stowe, Vermont:
I WAS SOMEBODY.
WHO, IS NO BUSINESS OF YOURS.

In a Georgia cemetery:
I TOLD YOU I WAS SICK!

John Penny's epitaph in the Wimborne, England, cemetery:
READER, IF CASH THOU ART
IN WANT OF ANY,
DIG 4 FEET DEEP
AND THOU WILT FIND A PENNY.

On Margaret Daniels' grave at Hollywood Cemetery Richmond, Virginia:
SHE ALWAYS SAID HER FEET WERE KILLING HER
BUT NOBODY BELIEVED HER.

In a cemetery in Hartscombe, England:
ON THE 22ND OF JUNE
JONATHAN FIDDLE
WENT OUT OF TUNE.

✹

Anna Hopewell's grave in Enosburg Falls, Vermont has an epitaph that sounds like something from a Three Stooges movie:
HERE LIES THE BODY OF OUR ANNA
DONE TO DEATH BY A BANANA
IT WASN'T THE FRUIT THAT LAID HER LOW
BUT THE SKIN OF THE THING THAT MADE HER GO.

✹

More fun with names with Owen Moore in Battersea, London, England:
GONE AWAY
OWIN' MORE
THAN HE COULD PAY.

✹

Someone in Winslow, Maine didn't like Mr. Wood:
IN MEMORY OF BEZA WOOD
DEPARTED THIS LIFE NOV. 2, 1837
AGED 45 YRS.
HERE LIES ONE WOOD ENCLOSED IN WOOD
ONE WOOD WITHIN ANOTHER.
THE OUTER WOOD IS VERY GOOD:
WE CANNOT PRAISE THE OTHER.

✹

On a grave from the 1880s in Nantucket, Massachusetts:
UNDER THE SOD AND UNDER THE TREES
LIES THE BODY OF JONATHAN PEASE.
HE IS NOT HERE, THERE'S ONLY THE POD:
PEASE SHELLED OUT AND WENT TO GOD.

The grave of Ellen Shannon in Girard, Pennsylvania
serves as a consumer warning:
WHO WAS FATALLY BURNED MARCH 21, 1870 BY THE
EXPLOSION OF A LAMP FILLED WITH
"R.E. DANFORTH'S NON-EXPLOSIVE BURNING FLUID"

Harry Edsel Smith of Albany, New York:
BORN 1903—DIED 1942
LOOKED UP THE ELEVATOR SHAFT TO SEE IF THE CAR
WAS ON THE WAY DOWN.
IT WAS.

In a Thurmont, Maryland, cemetery:
HERE LIES AN ATHEIST
ALL DRESSED UP
AND NO PLACE TO GO.

DR. FRED ROBERTS
BROOKLAND, ARKANSAS: OFFICE UPSTAIRS

HERE LIES ONE WHO FOR MEDICINE
WOULD NOT GIVE A LITTLE GOLD,
AND SO HIS LIFE HE LOST:
I BET NOW HE'D WISH AGAIN TO LIVE,
COULD HE BUT GUESS HOW MUCH HIS FUNERAL COST.

GOOD FRIEND FOR JESUS SAKE FORBEARE,
TO DIGG THE DUST ENCLOASED HEARE!
BLEST BE THE MAN THAT SPARES THES STONES,
AND CURST BE HE THAT MOVES MY BONES.
WILLIAM SHAKESPEARE
(Holy Trinity Church; Stratford-on-Avon, England)

Edward Elliot

Fairview Lawn Cemetery,

Hailifax, Nova Scotia
SACRED TO THE MEMORY OF
EVERETT EDWARD ELLIOTT
OF THE HEROIC CREW S.S. "TITANIC"
DIED ON DUTY APRIL 15, 1912
AGE 24 YEARS EACH MAN STOOD AT HIS POST
WHILE ALL THE WEAKER ONES WENT BY,
AND SHOWED ONCE MORE TO ALL THE WORLD
HOW ENGLISHMEN SHOULD DIE.

Thomas O. Murphy

Mountain View Cemetery,

Vancouver, British Columbia
SH-H-H

Christopher Wren

St. Paul's Cathedral,

London, England
IF YOU SEEK MY MONUMENT,
LOOK AROUND YOU

Wife of Peter Leslie
Greyfriar's Churchyard,
Edinburgh, Scotland
SHE WAS!
BUT WORDS ARE WANTING TO SAY WHAT.
THINK WHAT A WIFE SHOULD BE,
AND SHE WAS THAT.

This is on a tombstone in the old Irwin Cemetary near the old gold
& silver mining camp of Irwin, near Crested Butte, Colorado, and is
quite famous. The exact epitaph is on a stone in the cemetary at Como,
Colorado, in Park County off of highway 285 in South Park.
MY DEAR FRIENDS AS YOU PASS BY
AS YOU ARE NOW, SO ONCE WAS I.
AS I AM NOW, YOU SOON MUST BE.
PREPARE YOURSELVES TO FOLLOW ME.

CHAPTER ASSIGNMENT:

Write down what you would like for YOUR epitaph!

_____

_____

_____

_____

_____

_____

The Rice Family Tree

CHAPTER 20

The Tree Of Life

Now that you have finished reading this collection of inspiring stories about genealogists climbing their family trees, you've tasted some very sweet fruit in those trees. This last chapter is now yours to write! You may have the best story yet as you climb your own family tree.

Hopefully by now you have completed the chapter-end assignments. If you haven't, because you were so entranced with these wonderful stories that you couldn't put the book down, you can now begin to work on these tasks.

+ Start by collecting your own documents.
+ Gather and organize your photographs.
+ Complete a family group sheet with you as both child and parent.
+ Complete a family group sheet for your parents as children.
+ Complete a family group sheet for your own siblings as parents.
+ Write out a four generation pedigree as far as you can go. The blank spaces will show you where you can begin active research.

- Decide which ancestor you want to begin with. List which records will help you find the information you need.
- Choose a current relative you'd like to interview.
- Begin to explore the internet with the many resources listed in this book.
- Choose some family activities you'd like to do with your immediate family to get them involved in the process of discovering their family heritage.
- Begin to write your autobiography or update your personal journal.
- Choose who you will write a biography for in your family. Write out your plan for questions to ask and the method you will use to interview them.
- Create an address book for all your living family members of a certain ancestor.
- Create a descendants list from a chosen ancestor.
- Plan to attend or organize a family reunion this next year.
- Join a genealogical society or website surname list.
- Send us your own miraculous story of success as you survey your own view from the top!

Once you become hooked on genealogy you can be called an official tree hugger! To research your family's history is to dance through the generations of time while holding the hands of loved ones both on earth and in heaven. It is an honor and a privilege to unite those in mortality with those who have already made the next step into eternity. The tree of life is a universal motif, found in every ancient culture—a symbol of the uniting of heaven and earth. Your family tree is a living, growing part of you.

We hope that this book has given you some new tools to help you climb your family tree and that you will hear the whispers in the leaves as your ancestors join you in your efforts.

We weren't able to include in this one book all of the inspiring stories we received from contributors, so we have created a genealogy BLOG where you can read more amazing experiences, as well as submit your own! Go to **www.climbingfamilytrees.blogspot.com.**

Be sure to visit our main website at **www.climbingfamilytrees.com** to see the famous Howland family pedigree chart that shows how some famous people in history are related, including several presidents of the United States! A lot of other fun surprises await you there too. Now, enough reading . . . go get your hands dirty and discover your roots!

About the Authors

Trina Bates Boice (on right in picture) grew up in sunny California and later braved the cold and snow at Brigham Young University where she earned two Bachelor's degrees. While there she competed on the BYU Speech & Debate team, and BYU Ballroom Dance Team. She was President of the National Honor Society Phi Eta Sigma and ASBYU Secretary of Student Community Services.

Trina also studied at the University of Salamanca in Spain and later returned to serve a full-time mission to Madrid, Spain for the Church of Jesus Christ of Latter-day Saints. She earned a Master's degree from California College for Health Sciences. She worked as a Legislative Assistant for a Congressman in Washington D.C. and wrote a column called "The Boice Box" for a local newspaper in Georgia where she lived for 15 years. She has a real estate license, travel agent license, a Black Belt in Tae Kwon Do, and helps her husband, Tom, with their real estate appraisal and investment companies.

Trina was honored in November 2004 as George Bush's "Points of Light Volunteer" and also received the President's Lifetime Volunteer Service award. She was the "2004 Honor Young Mother of the Year" for the state of California and lives in beautiful Carlsbad with her four wonderful sons. They keep busy with Scouting, all kinds of sports, and are surfer wannabes now that they live closer to the beach. They now brave the cold and snow of Utah together to go skiing and visit family!

Tracey Bates Long (on left in picture) has always loved climbing trees. From climbing beautiful oak trees in California where she grew up, to trees of knowledge at Brigham Young University where she graduated in Nursing and Spanish, she can be found in trees. In between hiding in the library to climb family trees while at BYU, she also competed on the Speech and Debate team and toured with the Ballroom Dance Company.

She discovered the beautiful rain forest trees of Colombia where she served as a full time missionary for the Church of Jesus Christ of Latter-Day Saints. Upon her return she married Larry Long with whom she is TREEmendously in love. She earned a Masters Degree in Health Education from California College for Health Sciences and is a Certified Diabetes Educator. She currently teaches Nursing part-time at both the University of Nevada Las Vegas and the Community College of Southern Nevada. She has drawn a lot of crayon trees while teaching preschool for 12 years and serving on the PTA board.

She and her husband have 6 TREEiffic children and reside in the cactus tree desert of Las Vegas, where she climbs trees teaching Family History. She claims to have traced her genealogy back to Adam and Eve, Derryberry that is!

About the Illustrator

Calvin W. Boice III made a flashy entrance into the world by being born at home on Friday the 13th! His parents were trying to get to the hospital, but Calvin just couldn't wait to start his life. He was named after his grandfather and great-grandfather when his mom gratefully told his dad, "You can name your son anything you want, since you delivered him!"

Calvin has won several art contests at school and in the community. He runs on the Cross Country and Track teams at Carlsbad High School as a Sophomore and is a straight A student. He earned his Eagle Scout award, and after climbing Mount Whitney, the highest mountain in the continental United States, he earned the 50 Miler Award from the Boy Scouts of America.

In 2004 Calvin earned the Presidential Volunteer Service Award for his service at church, school, and in Scouting, as well as his efforts serving with "Operation Appreciation" for the military and "Supporting Urban Neighborhoods." He is listed in *Who's Who of American High School Students*.

He also received the Hometown USA Award presented by the Keep America Beautiful Foundation. Calvin lives with his family in Carlsbad, California.